OpenCart 1.4
Beginner's Guide

Build and manage professional online shopping stores
easily using OpenCart

Murat Yilmaz

BIRMINGHAM - MUMBAI

OpenCart 1.4
Beginner's Guide

First published: August 2010

Production Reference: 1190810

Published by Packt Publishing Ltd.
32 Lincoln Road
Olton
Birmingham, B27 6PA, UK.

ISBN 978-1-847193-02-9

www.packtpub.com

Cover Image by Duraid Fatouhi (duraidfatouhi@yahoo.com)

Credits

Author

Murat Yilmaz

Reviewers

Jose Argudo

Tomáš Kissík

René Skotnik

Acquisition Editor

Dilip Venkatesh

Development Editor

Akash Johari

Technical Editor

Pallavi Kachare

Indexer

Tejal Daruwale

Editorial Team Leader

Akshara Aware

Project Team Leader

Priya Mukherji

Project Coordinator

Leena Purkait

Proofreader

Aaron Nash

Production Coordinator

Melwyn D'sa

Cover Work

Melwyn D'sa

About the author

Murat Yilmaz is a software developer, and online entrepreneur who lives in Moscow. Murat has over 10 years of experience in different IT fields including development of web driven solutions, database and OLAP systems and has worked in several international companies in Istanbul (Turkey), Anchorage (Alaska), and Moscow (Russia) as a consultant. He currently runs his own blog and online advertising network. He holds a bachelor degree in Computer Science, Marmara University at Istanbul. He spends his free time playing progressive rock songs on the guitar and enjoys writing for his gadgets and technology blog at www.vubx.com.

He is also author of OpenX Ad Server Beginner's Guide from Packt, which teaches people about building and maintaining professional, online advertising solutions for their web sites.

For my newborn son Deniz, I wish that your life will always be full of sunshine and a blue sea of dreams.

About the reviewers

Jose Argudo is a web developer from Valencia, Spain. After finishing his studies he started working for a web design company. After working six years for that company, and some others, he decided to start working as a freelancer.

Now, after some years have passed, he things that's the best decision he has ever taken, a decision that has let him work with the tools he likes, such as Codeigniter, Joomla!, Cakephp, Jquery, and other well known open source technologies.

For the last months he has also been reviewing some Pack Publications books, like Magento 1.3 Sales Tactics, Openx Ad server, Joomla! 1.5 Beginners Guide and many more.

He has also been author of the Codeigniter 1.7 book, and is now working on a Joomla! book that will soon be finished.

To my girlfriend Silvia whose support helps me every day.

Tomáš Kissík is Slovak republic citizen; he studies informatics and economy in Czech Republic. He works with web technologies, PHP, and CMS systems for five years.

I want to thank for the support of my family, friends, and people from the Opencart community.

Table of Contents

Preface

OpenCart is a popular open source shopping cart solution and provides elegantly written tools to establish a fully functional online store from scratch in a very short time with intuitive screens.

On the other hand, it can be a difficult task for beginners to go beyond the basics and apply all the features which they will require for their business.

This practical book gives you hands-on experience of using and managing OpenCart, helping you start feature-rich, professional online stores easily. It also teaches you how to organize your online store effectively in terms of products, payments, shipping, orders, and customer relations.

What this book covers

Chapter 1, *Installing OpenCart* shows a step-by-step installation of OpenCart store on a hosting by emphasizing the important points that require extra attention. These include understanding the system requirements before installation, setting file, folder permissions of OpenCart files, creating a database for the store, and completing the installation with the wizard.

Chapter 2, *Categories, Products and Options* shows different ways of organizing an online store after introducing the reader important terms. This is followed by hands-on examples on adding categories, subcategories, brand definitions, product information with images. Then, the chapter dives into details of extending a simple product with option features for customers to buy.

Chapter 3, *Tax Management* provides in-depth information about one of the most essential elements of every online store, taxes. The chapter introduces Geo Zone, Tax Class terms and how to apply taxes according to shipping addresses of customers. Throughout the chapter, the reader will learn how to add geo zones, assign geo zones to tax classes and choose correct tax class for products. The chapter ends with samples on displaying prices without taxes on front-page and show them only on checkout pages as a final price.

Chapter 4, *Configuring Store Settings* first gives the basic information about configuring essential store information including setting default local settings. After that, the information is extended by activation of SEO support, application of SEO (search engine optimization) on categories, product pages with detailed hands-on examples. The chapter continues to explain how to install new templates, activating different modules such as Google Talk for online help functionality. The chapter ends with the application of other important modules like Privacy policy, terms and conditions.

Chapter 5, *Setting Payment Models* explains, with the help of a diagram, a typical online credit card process by emphasizing all important sections. The chapter continues to explain what merchant accounts, payment gateways are. Throughout the chapter, the most famous and widely used payment gateway, PayPal is very thoroughly investigated by many hands-on examples and is shown how to integrate different PayPal services (Standard and Pro versions) to a store according to individual needs. The chapter ends with applied examples on configuring bank transfer, cash on delivery, cheque/money order.

Chapter 6, *Setting Shipping Methods* is all about configuring and enabling the most modern shipping methods for store customers. The chapter starts with a section which shows how to limit shipment to certain countries/regions. The chapter continues with examples on setting free shipping, flat rate shipping, per item shipping, weight based shipping methods. Finally, two of the popular shipping services UPS (United Parcel Service) and USPS (United States Postal Service) are discussed in detail with examples.

Chapter 7, *Offering Coupons Discounts* explains what kind of coupons for customers are supported by OpenCart. These include percentage based, fixed amount and with free shipping coupons. We will then learn how to apply discounts for selected products for a period of time as a way of promotion. Finally, it is shown how to activate wholesale discount for bulk purchases. At the end of this chapter, the reader will have a strong knowledge on coupons and how to correctly activate them according to store's detailed requirements.

Chapter 8, *Understanding Order Lifecycle* explains whole process of online orders as a flowchart at the beginning. This enables readers to see the whole picture of what is going on at each step of order management. Then, the chapter explains how orders are tracked on administration panel and by customers on storefront. The chapter continues with an explanation on generating invoices. Finally, it shows how to change order statuses manually according to process of handling the order. Some sample order statuses discussed are pending, processing, shipped, completed, cancelled.

Chapter 9, *Managing Customers and Users* starts with important discussion on why customer registration has advantages and how to set important customer related store settings. The chapter continues with hands-on example on grouping customers according to activity, such as VIP or high income customers. We will learn how to optimize customer relationships of a store by sending regular email newsletters and direct messages. Finally, the chapter discusses how to optimize the backend administration by opening new user groups, assigning users to groups with different permissions (such as a person only deals with orders while another one only changes/enters information about products).

Chapter 10, *Localization* provides essential information on how to find and download different language packs for the store, uploading language packs, changing individual language texts, adding new currencies, and updating them according to the latest exchange rates each day automatically.

Chapter 11, *Upgrading OpenCart* will teach the reader how to make backups of a running OpenCart store, downloading latest version, uploading the new files to a hosting server, running the upgrade script, checking the newly updated store and finally information about how to restore to the old version if upgrade fails or has serious problems.

What you need for this book

The book doesn't require any advanced IT skills. Basic computer and IT skills are enough to be able to follow the book easily. All extra information regarding usage of several online services, tools are given with clear illustrations and step by step instructions.

Who this book is for

This book is aimed at individuals who want to develop professional online stores without any hands-on programming experience, and clients/non-developers who will be managing their inventory and processing orders through the back end.

Conventions

In this book, you will find a number of styles of text that distinguish between different kinds of information. Here are some examples of these styles, and an explanation of their meaning.

Code words in text are shown as follows: "Change the destination directory as `/public/html/` and click on Move File(s) button".

New terms and **important words** are shown in bold. Words that you see on the screen, in menus or dialog boxes for example, appear in the text like this: "Let's click on the link and choose the **Save File** option to save it in the computer".

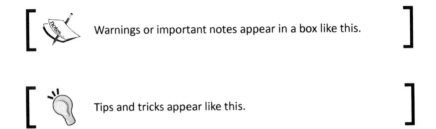

Warnings or important notes appear in a box like this.

Tips and tricks appear like this.

Reader feedback

Feedback from our readers is always welcome. Let us know what you think about this book—what you liked or may have disliked. Reader feedback is important for us to develop titles that you really get the most out of.

To send us general feedback, simply send an e-mail to feedback@packtpub.com, and mention the book title via the subject of your message.

If there is a book that you need and would like to see us publish, please send us a note in the **SUGGEST A TITLE** form on www.packtpub.com or e-mail suggest@packtpub.com.

If there is a topic that you have expertise in and you are interested in either writing or contributing to a book, see our author guide on www.packtpub.com/authors.

Customer support

Now that you are the proud owner of a Packt book, we have a number of things to help you to get the most from your purchase.

Errata

Although we have taken every care to ensure the accuracy of our content, mistakes do happen. If you find a mistake in one of our books—maybe a mistake in the text or the code—we would be grateful if you would report this to us. By doing so, you can save other readers from frustration and help us improve subsequent versions of this book. If you find any errata, please report them by visiting http://www.packtpub.com/support, selecting your book, clicking on the errata submission form link, and entering the details of your errata. Once your errata are verified, your submission will be accepted and the errata will be uploaded on our website, or added to any list of existing errata, under the Errata section of that title. Any existing errata can be viewed by selecting your title from http://www.packtpub.com/support.

Piracy

Piracy of copyright material on the Internet is an ongoing problem across all media. At Packt, we take the protection of our copyright and licenses very seriously. If you come across any illegal copies of our works, in any form, on the Internet, please provide us with the location address or website name immediately so that we can pursue a remedy.

Please contact us at copyright@packtpub.com with a link to the suspected pirated material.

We appreciate your help in protecting our authors, and our ability to bring you valuable content.

Questions

You can contact us at questions@packtpub.com if you are having a problem with any aspect of the book, and we will do our best to address it.

1
Installing OpenCart

Since OpenCart is a considerably new online shopping cart solution, many web hosting service providers do not have one-click installation for OpenCart yet. So, we will need to install OpenCart ourselves.

Installation of OpenCart is an easy task and follows a standard procedure like PHP and MySQL-based open source software. On the other hand, there are some important key points we should be careful at.

In this chapter we shall:

- ◆ Learn the system requirements needed to install OpenCart
- ◆ Learn to download and upload OpenCart files to a web server
- ◆ Learn to set file and folder permissions
- ◆ Learn to create a MySQL database and user
- ◆ Learn to complete installation with the OpenCart wizard

This chapter is suggested for reading even if you are a tech-savvy computer user, as you can eliminate the possible problems while installing OpenCart.

System requirements

By the time of the writing of this book, the latest OpenCart release is 1.4.7 and the system requirements are valid for this version. Previous versions can need the same or fewer requirements.

We would suggest installing v1.4.7 and reading the book carefully. If there are new releases of OpenCart after the publication of this book, you can at any time download it from the OpenCart website and see the differences easily because you will already have a strong foundation in OpenCart after completing the book.

We must download and install OpenCart on our own or on a shared web hosting solution. OpenCart system can run on an Apache or Windows server. Currently, OpenCart supports only MySQL database. Overall, OpenCart was designed to work flawlessly on an ideal LAMP solution (Linux, Apache, MySql, and PHP), but it is also possible to run using a Windows server, MySQL, and PHP.

 If you aim to run OpenCart on Windows, you can use WAMP Server. It is available for download at http://www.wampserver.com/en/.

The following screenshot shows the minimum system requirements for OpenCart for installation and running without problems.

You should contact your hosting provider if you are not sure whether these settings are set or not.

PHP Settings	Required Settings
PHP Version:	5.0+
Register Globals:	Off
Magic Quotes GPC:	Off
File Uploads:	On
Session Auto Start:	Off

Extension	Required Settings
MySQL:	On
GD:	On
cURL:	On
ZIP:	On

 If you want to take advantage of SEO URLs, your hosting should allow using mod_rewrite extension for Apache and permission to change .htaccess file

We will talk about SEO in OpenCart in Chapter 4, *Configuring Store Settings*.

Installing OpenCart

Be sure that your web hosting solution meets the previous requirements before starting installation steps. The easiest way of determining this is to send a requirement list to web server technical support. We will complete installing OpenCart using the following sections:

♦ Downloading OpenCart from `http://opencart.com`
♦ Uploading OpenCart files to a web host
♦ Creating MySQL database and a user for OpenCart
♦ Using OpenCart installation wizard
♦ Deleting installation files after completion
♦ Browsing to online storefront
♦ Making first login to OpenCart administration interface

Now, let's start to explore each section in detail.

Downloading OpenCart

Downloading the latest version of OpenCart is an easy and straightforward task. Let's see how we achieve downloading.

Time for action – downloading OpenCart

In this section, we are going to download OpenCart archive file.

1. We browse to the `http://www.opencart.com/index.php?route=download/download` link. This page will list the latest OpenCart version. The download page is similar to the following screenshot.

 We can see the full list of OpenCart versions on: `http://code.google.com/p/opencart/`.

2. Let's click on the link and choose the **Save File** option to save it in the computer:

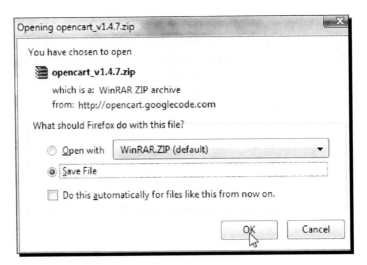

What just happened?

We have downloaded the OpenCart files as a ZIP archive file on our computer. Now we are ready to upload the files to the web host.

Uploading OpenCart files

There are two common methods for uploading files to a web host:

- Using cPanel File Manager Utility
- Using an FTP Client

We will learn both the methods with examples.

The first method is suggested because we can upload the installation files **faster** to the host.

We suggest installing OpenCart on a directory, such as `http://yourwebsite.com/store`

By doing this, we will able to close the shop temporarily if we need to later, without affecting the root domain at `http://yourwebsite.com`.

Let's start with the suggested cPanel method.

Time for action – uploading OpenCart using cPanel File Manager

This is the first method of uploading OpenCart files to a web host. Many modern web hosting solutions include a control panel called cPanel, and we can use the cPanel File Manager utility to directly upload a ZIP file to web host and decompress the files there easily.

In this example, we will install OpenCart on the **store** directory.

 You can generally reach cPanel on `http://yourwebsite.com/cpanel` with the username and password which the hosting provider emailed to you upon registration.

1. Let's open **File Manager** utility at cPanel.

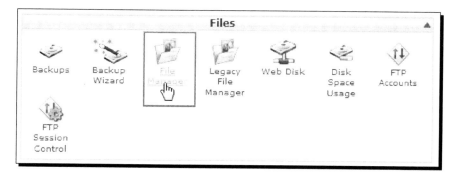

2. It will choose the Web Root as default. We will continue with the **Go** button.

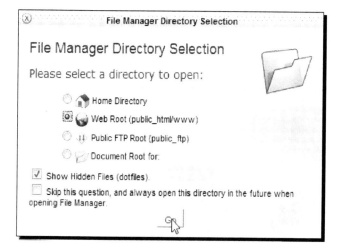

3. Let's click on the **Upload** link.

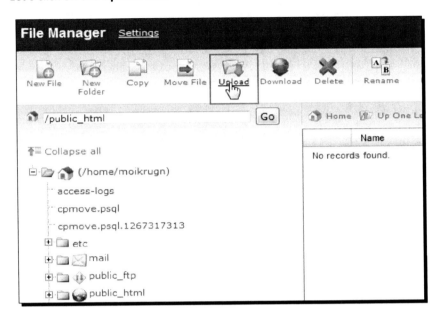

4. Let's choose OpenCart ZIP file using the **Browse** button on the next screen. After the upload completes, we return back to the main cPanel File Manager screen.

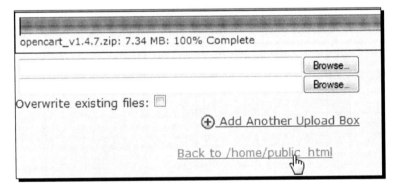

5. We will right-click on the file and select **Extract**.

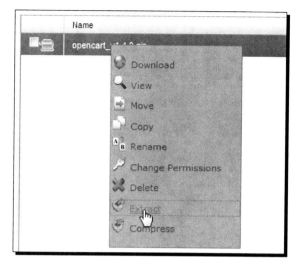

6. It will open a pop-up window. Just press the **Extract File(s)** button to decompress the ZIP file into the root web folder.

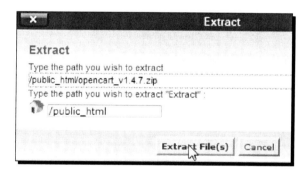

All files were extracted into a folder named `opencart_v1.7`.

 The default folder name depends on our OpenCart version.

7. We will need to browse into this folder first. We see a folder called **upload** under it. We will need to rename it as **store** at first.

Right-click on it and choose **Rename** from the menu.

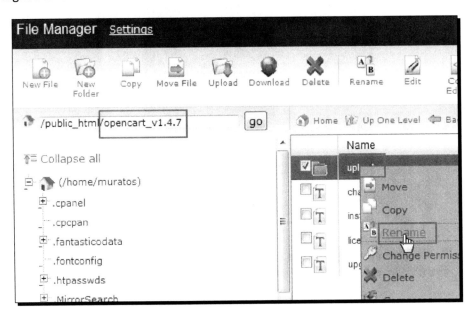

8. Rename the directory as **store**, as in the following screenshot:

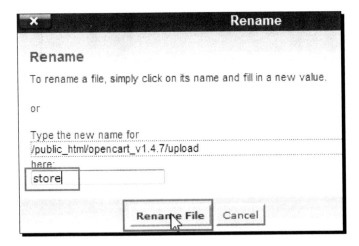

9. We will need to move the renamed store directory to the root. Let's right-click on the **store** directory and choose **Move** from the menu.

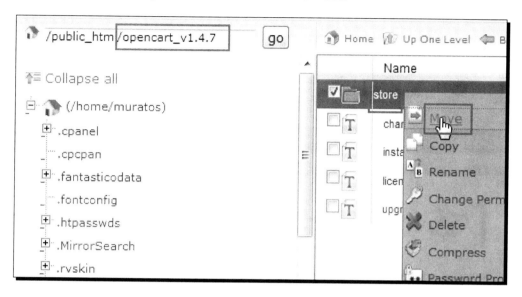

10. Change the destination directory as /public_html/ and click on Move File(s) button.

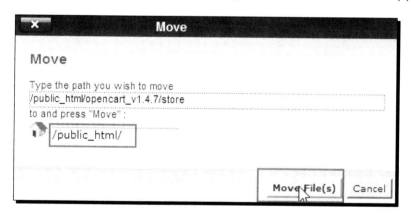

What just happened?

OpenCart files are now on the web host in a subdirectory. Our online store will be reachable at `http://yourwebsite.com/store` after completion of all the remaining installation steps.

 If you have completed uploading OpenCart files to a subdirectory using cPanel File Manager tool already, skip the following action and continue reading Setting File Permissions.

Time for action – uploading OpenCart using an FTP Client

This is the second method of uploading files to a webserver.

 If you have already used the first method (Uploading Files using cPanel) please skip this action and continue with Setting File Permissions.

In this section, we will learn how to decompress the OpenCart files in a local folder and upload to the root of web server using an FTP Client.

1. Right-click on the previously downloaded OpenCart file on your computer and click **Extract Here** option.

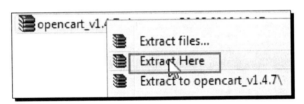

As a result, we will have a folder named `opencart_v1.7` with the structured folders and files inside.

 Please note that folder name can be different depending on the OpenCart version we downloaded.

2. We will create a directory named as **store** on the root of the website using the ftp **Make Directory** command.

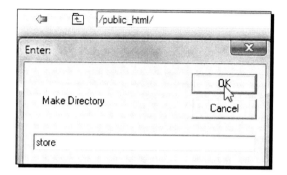

3. Upload all the files and the subfolders in `opencart_v1.7/upload` folder to the web host in the`/store` folder. We use a free FTP client software called CoreFTP, which can be downloaded at `http://www.coreftp.com/`. Choose all the files and folders in the directory from the left panel and drag and drop into the right panel where the web root folder exists. In most cases, it is /www folder. So, our destination is /www/store.

The following screenshot shows the process before dragging and droping the files:

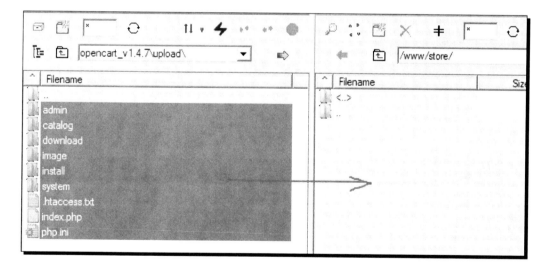

And the screenshot after uploading the files to the folder named as **store** is as follows:

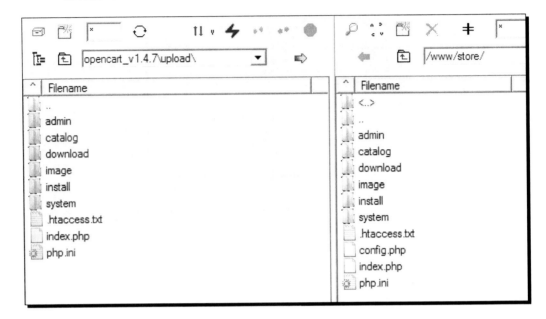

Notice that it is a time consuming process since there are many files in OpenCart system. Let's wait until all the files are uploaded to the web server.

What just happened?

We have uploaded all OpenCart files and subfolders to the store directory on the website using an ftp client.

So, our online store will be reachable at `http://yourwebsite.com/store` after completion of all installation steps.

Pop quiz – Uploading OpenCart Files

Suppose that we have a very slow internet connection and want to install OpenCart on a web host without any possible interruptions on file transfer. Which upload method is more effective in terms of speed and reliability?

1. Using an FTP Client program.
2. Using cPanel File Transfer Utility.

Time for action – setting file permissions

OpenCart system uses its several directories dynamically to create, change, and delete the files when needed. Because of this, we have to be sure that the correct file permissions are applied on these files and folders.

Now, let's see how we will set the permissions using cPanel File Manager:

1. We should be sure that the following directories and config files are writeable, meaning that their permissions are set to at least 755. We can check this by using cPanel file manager.

- ❑ /store/image
- ❑ /store/image/cache
- ❑ /store/image/data
- ❑ /store/system/cache
- ❑ /store/system/logs
- ❑ /store/download
- ❑ /store/config.php
- ❑ /store/admin/config.php

Some hosting systems require 777 permissions for OpenCart to work properly. If the installation screens which we will soon learn give such unwritable errors, then we should set permissions to 777 and try going through with the installation screen again.

The following screenshot shows that all these directories are set to 755 properly, but `config.php` file is not set to 755:

📁	admin	4 KB	httpd/unix-directory	0755
📁	catalog	4 KB	httpd/unix-directory	0755
📁	download	4 KB	httpd/unix-directory	0755
📁	image	4 KB	httpd/unix-directory	0755
📁	install	4 KB	httpd/unix-directory	0755
📁	system	4 KB	httpd/unix-directory	0755
T	.htaccess.txt	389 Bytes	text/plain	0644
PHP	config.php	0 Bytes	application/x-httpd-php	0644
PHP	index.php	5.51 KB	application/x-httpd-php	0644
	php.ini	293 Bytes	text/x-generic	0644

2. So, let's open cPanel file manager and right-click on `config.php` file. Let's select **Change Permissions:**

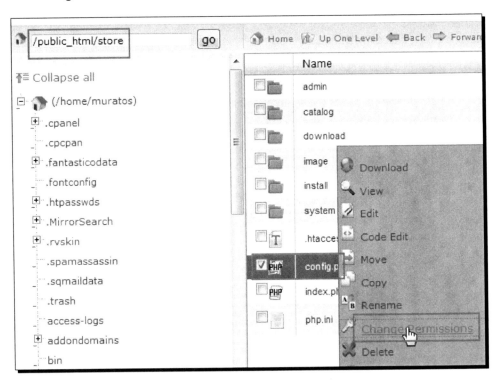

3. Set Permission level to **755**. Click the **Change Permissions** button.

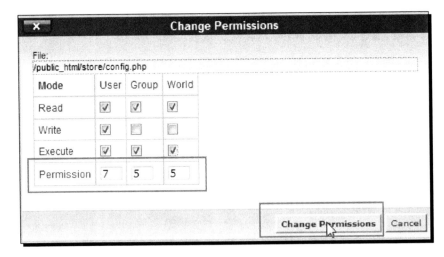

4. We must repeat this process for all the folders listed below including the subfolders and files inside one by one if not set correctly to 755:

- /store/image
- /store/image/cache
- /store/image/data
- /store/system/cache
- /store/system/logs
- /store/download
- /store/config.php
- /store/admin/config.php

What just happened?

We have set the needed file and folder permissions to 755. It was needed for OpenCart to install and operate correctly. Depending on our hosting provider's linux settings, we might need 777 as well.

 Curious readers can learn more about server security on this `http://www.unix.com/unix-dummies-questions-answers/33137-chmod-777-security-risks.html` link.

Time for action – creating a MySQL database and user

This step is needed for OpenCart to connect and store all the data in a MySQL database. We will learn how to create a new database and user for this database. We will later use this information in OpenCart Installation wizard.

We will use MySQL Databases link on cPanel. Even though there can be slight differences on different cPanel versions, the main idea and the process is the same.

1. Click on **MySQL Databases** link on cPanel:

2. Enter a name for the database. Here, we named the database as **opencart**. Then, click on the **Create Database** button.

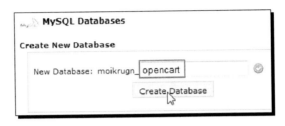

If we are on a share hosting, a prefix will be added automatically to the name we provided. This is generally the username which we use to log in to the cPanel. So, your database name will follow the template of cPanelLogin_databasename.

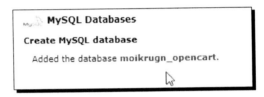

Take a note of the database name including the prefix.

3. Now, let's create a user and assign this user to our newly created database. We go back from database creation result page and jump to MySQL Users section.

Choose a **username** and **password**. Repeat the **password** on the last text box and be sure that the password is not very easy to guess for security preferably a mixture of letters and numbers.) We have chosen **dbuser** as the username. Click on the **Create User** button after filling all the required textboxes.

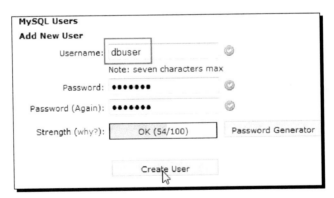

Please note that a prefix will be added to the user as well. Take a note of the username.

4. We need to add user to the database as the last step. Choose the newly created user and database for OpenCart, and then click the **Add** button.

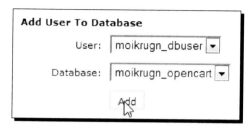

5. In this step, we are going to assign privileges for the user in the database. Select the **All Privileges** option, and then press the **Make Changes** button to give all the privileges to the user.

Providing all MySQL privileges to a user can be dangerous on a production site. Optionally, you can remove unnecessary permissions such as create, drop, and alter tables after installation is complete. Also note that some plugins which we can later install can require create, and alter permissions.

Depending on our knowledge and experience on MySQL permissions, we are free to choose an advanced or simplified privileges management.

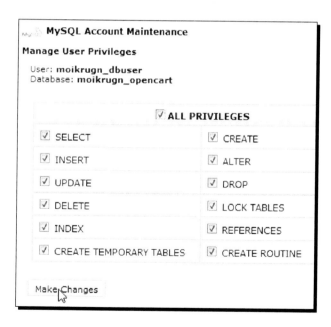

The following screenshot shows the result page after clicking the **Make Changes** button:

 MySQL® Database Wizard

User moikrugn_dbuser was added to the database moikrugn_opencart.

[Go Back]

What just happened?

We have seen how to prepare a database for OpenCart. The steps include:

1. Choosing a name for the database.
2. Choosing a username and providing a secure password.
3. Adding user to the database.
4. Adding privileges to user for the database.

Now we are ready to continue our installation by using OpenCart Installation Wizard.

Time for action – using OpenCart Installation Wizard

1. Let's browse the domain name where we put OpenCart files. In our example, it is `http://yourwebsite.com/store`. You should use your own OpenCart path. We will be redirected to a License screen automatically. Click **Continue** to start.

2. OpenCart will control several installation requirements, including PHP settings and extensions.

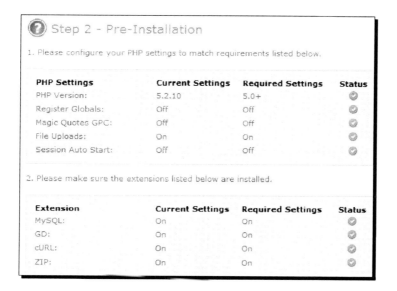

3. Then, the permissions of several files and directories are checked. If there are no errors, all we have to do is click the **Continue** button.

If the system check finds any serious error, it will stop the installation temporarily and will not let us go further until we solve the problem. If it is the case, please check the requirements list section and file permission settings again carefully. If there is a need to make changes on the PHP settings and extension, please contact your hosting provider.

4. In this step, we will supply the database connection information to OpenCart system. First, we should provide the previously created MySQL user and password for **User** and **Password** fields. Then, fill the MySQL database name in the **Database Name** field.

Finally, we should choose a **Username**, **Password,** and **Email** to be used to log in and manage the OpenCart system.

Let's ignore the **Database Prefix** option.

If we are allowed to create only one MySQL database for all applications being installed on hosting, it is a good idea to use Database Prefix option. It would put the shortened text in front of table names which will help us in differentiating tables in each application. `oc` would be a good prefix example. So, the tables would look like `oc_tablename`.

"After filling in all the required fields, click on the **Continue** button.

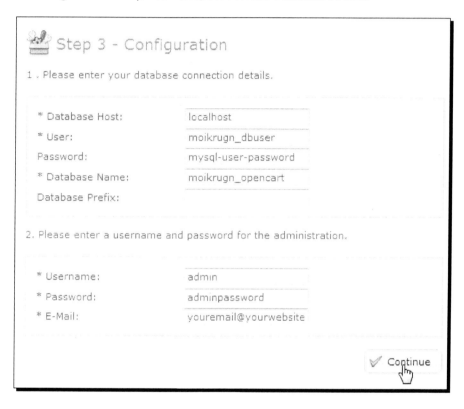

5. Even though the following screen has informed us that we have finished, we actually have not!

For security purposes, we must delete the installation directory. Then, we should check the online storefront and administration screens to be sure that everything is working in the default settings.

6. Let's open cPanel file manager again and browse to **/store** folder. Let's find **install** folder. We will right-click on it and choose **Delete** from the menu.

We could also use an Ftp client to delete, store, or install folder.

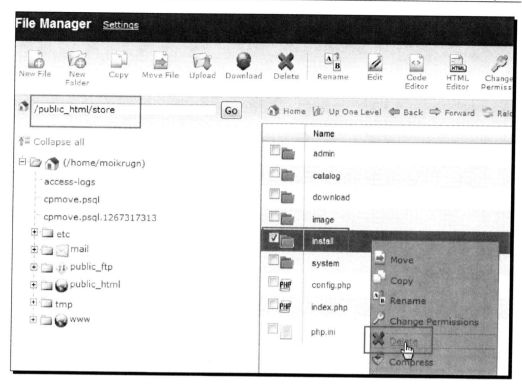

7. The next step is to confirm the deletion of the **install** folder. Let's click on the **Delete File(s)** button.

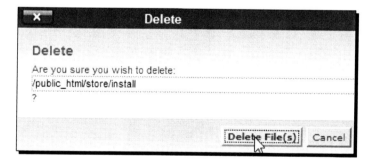

8. Let's browse to http://yourwebsite.com/store, the online shop storefront. We can see a pre-populated sample store that is similar to the following screenshot:

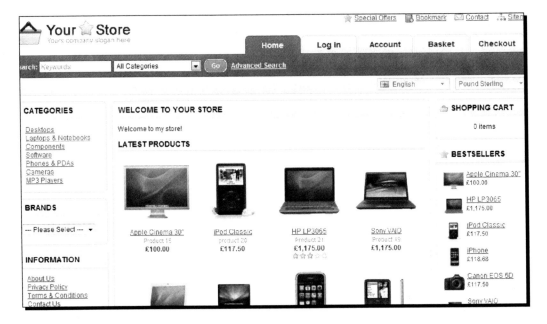

Let's browse to the OpenCart administration screen at http://yourwebsite.com/store/admin and log in by using our admin **username** and **password**.

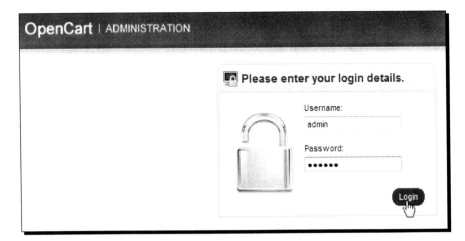

We will see an administration screen similar to the following screenshot:

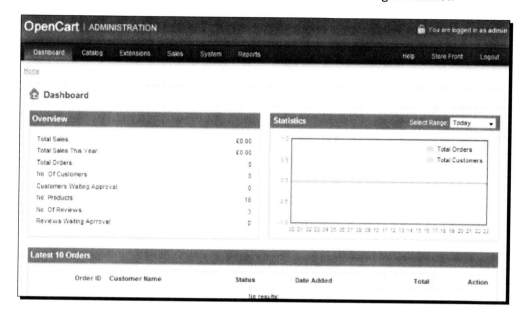

Congratulations! Our OpenCart installation is now complete.

What just happened?

We have completed the installation using OpenCart wizard. The steps included the approval of license agreement, system checks (php settings, file permissions), providing database connection information, and deleting the install folder after completion of install. Finally, there are checking the storefront and administration screens.

We have now a sample running OpenCart system.

Have a go hero – Adding another OpenCart instance

Now, it is time for testing your skills on installing another instance of OpenCart at the `http://yourwebsite.com/teststore` folder. Later, will only be able to use this instance for testing purposes before applying some new things on the original store which we have together completed installing. Try to do the steps on your own without looking at the chapter sections at first. If difficulties occur, re-read the required chapter sections.

Summary

As you see, OpenCart installation is very straightforward. The most important thing is to be sure that your hosting environment runs on an Apache server with (Linux or Windows) and PHP 5.0+ and MySQL is supported. If we want to SEO-enable our system, let's be sure that `mod_rewrite` extension for Apache and permission to change `.htaccess` file is allowed.

In this chapter, we learned how to install OpenCart on a web server.

Specifically, we covered:

◆ Requirements

◆ Downloading and uploading files

◆ Setting permissions

◆ Creating MySQL database and user

◆ Using Installation Wizard

◆ Deleting install directory after the completion of installation

◆ Checking storefront and administration screens

We are ready to explore OpenCart categories and products and their options on the next chapter.

2

Categories, Products, and Options

An optimized organization of an online store mostly depends on the defined categories and subcategories. There are several ways to organize an online store. Before starting adding products, we should carefully plan how our store will be browsed by visitors using the categories and subcategories.

In this chapter we shall learn:

- The terms category, product, and option.
- Different possible scenarios when organizing a sample online shoe store
- Deleting pre-populated store data
- Adding categories and subcategories
- Adding manufacturers (brands)
- Adding a simple product with basic data
- Extending the product with feature options
- Adding extra images for a product

Category, product, and option

Before starting to add data for our store, let's understand the hierarchy amongst the terms such as category, product, and option.

Products are the items that are sold in our online store. **Categories** are a classification of very closely related products in groups. **Options** are the values which further define the properties of a product. Options enable the customers to choose different features for a certain product.

For example, for our shoe store, **a winter boot** would be a product in **men's shoes** or **women's shoes** category. The color of the boot is a typical option for customers to choose. So, **black color** is a sample **option value** for a winter boot.

In OpenCart, a product can be listed under multiple categories and can get many options as well.

Now, let's give four different sample category organizations for an online shoe store.

Category Organization #1

The following sample hierarchy shows a typical category organization for a large shoe store which sells every kind of shoe:

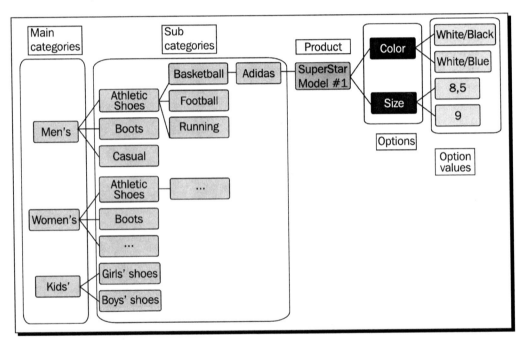

Category Organization #2

The following organization can suit a women fashion shoe store better, if most of the customers who visit this store care about the brand rather than shoe type and start browsing for a certain brand. Notice that we have used several brands as top categories:

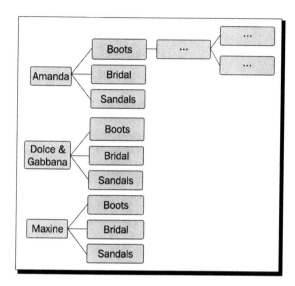

Category Organization #3

We could even define the size option as a category for a shoe store in addition to the typical categories. Note that it would complicate the backend management of the store since we would need to assign every size option for a shoe to a related shoe size category.

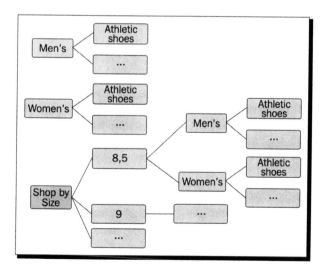

Category Organization #4

It is possible to make a category for a seasonal, very popular shoe brand. If your customers are heavily looking for UGGs, it is a good idea to make a category for it. For example, UGG brand shoes could even be a top category depending on the sales trends. We can later delete this specific category after the season finishes.

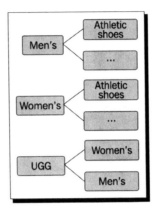

Overall, the correct store organization depends on how the majority of store visitors begin browsing on our store. The aim is to provide what they look for most, as easily as possible.

We will follow the traditional category organization throughout the book similar to the one in example #1.

Pre-installed store categories, products

As you can remember from Chapter 1, OpenCart installation had built a sample electronics store upon completion of installation.

It is a good idea to delete all the data before starting a fresh online store which we will customize according to our needs.

Time for action – deleting pre-installed store data

In this section, we will delete all the old sample store data that we will not need for our new store.

1. We browse to the OpenCart administration panel and make a login using the **username** and **password** we have created upon installation. The administration panel is available at `http://yourwebsite.com/store/admin`.

2. Let's click on the **Catalog | Categories** menu.

3. Let's choose all category items by using the checkbox on the top-left of the screen and then **delete** all categories.

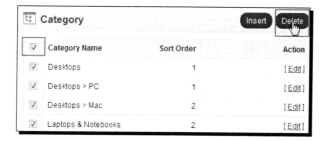

4. As a result, we have deleted all categories, as shown in the following screenshot:

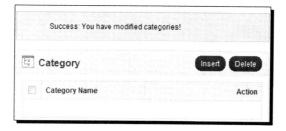

5. The next step is to browse a **Catalog | Products** menu.

6. We select all the products on the page by using the checkbox on the top-left of the screen and clicking the **Delete** button.

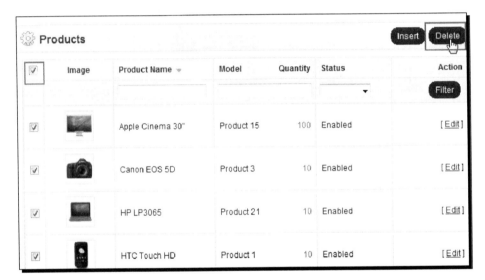

7. Do not forget to repeat this process for the second page to **delete** all products.

What just happened?

We have just finished deleting all categories and products on the pre-installed sample store.

Have a go hero – deleting pre-populated manufacturer data

Now, it is your turn to delete all manufacturer data which was inserted automatically upon installation.

 Hint: It is under the **Catalog | Manufacturers** menu.

Categories and subcategories

Categories and subcategories determine what kind of browsing experience we will provide to the visitors. Let's start adding a sample classical shoe store category organization.

Time for action – adding a category and subcategory under it

In this section, we will add Men's shoes as a parent (top) category for our store. Then, we will add a Athletic subcategory under it.

1. Let's open the **Catalog | Categories** menu.

2. We will click on the **Insert** button next.

3. Let's fill in the general category data similar to the following screenshot by **Category Name**, **Meta Tag Description**, and **Description**. Then we will click on the **Data** tab.

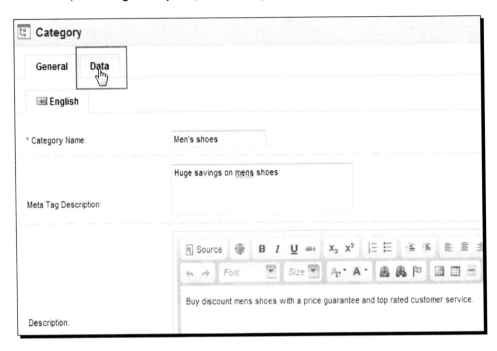

4. We should choose the **Default** store name from the **Stores** list and click on the **Save** button. We can disable a category showing in our store by changing **Category status**. The default value is **Enabled**. We can also arrange categories in a way that they will appear in the order we want using **Sort Order** field. By default, it is **0**.

    We will talk about **SEO Keyword** field in one of the later chapters. Leave the other fields on their default settings.

We can run more than one store on a single OpenCart installation. We will explore the topic of creating new stores in later chapters. For this chapter, we will be doing operations on Default installed store.

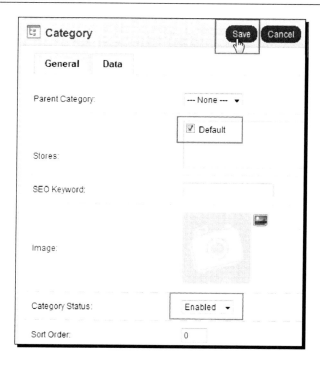

5. We have finished adding the **Men's shoes** category. Now, let's click on the **Insert** button to continue adding the subcategory.

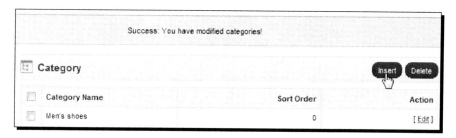

6. We fill in the general information for the **Athletic** subcategory similar to the following screenshot. Then, let's click on the **Data** tab.

7. We choose **Men's shoes** as **Parent Category** in order to place the Athletic category as a sub-category under Men's shoes. Let's choose **Default** store. We will click on the small icon on the **Image** field to add a new image for the category.

8. Image manager will be opened. We will see a list of pre-uploaded images for the sample store. Let's continue by clicking on the **New Folder** menu item. A pop-up box will be opened. Let's enter **shoes** as a new folder name and click on the **Submit** button.

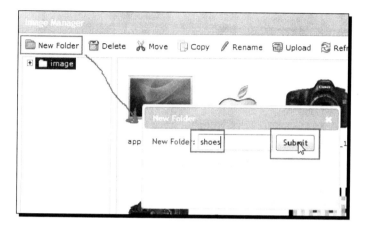

9. We have now **shoes** directory under the **image** directory. Let's click on the **Upload** menu item.

10. After we upload an image from the local computer, we will see that the image is available for usage. Let's double click on the image.

11. Finally, we have attached an image for the category. Let's click on the **Save** button to complete the process.

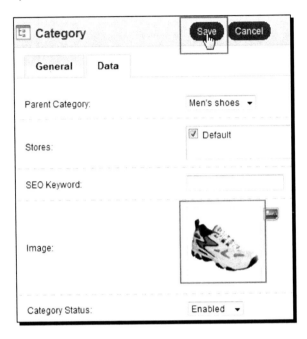

12. Let's browse to our store and browse the Men's shoes category. Notice that some of the information we have provided for these categories have appeared: the description field for men's shoes and image for Athletic sub-category.

What just happened?

We have added a Men's shoes category and Athletic subcategory under it. Notice that we have carefully written, detailed text in the meta description field for both categories. It is important to not neglect this field because search engines use meta HTML tag data to help indexing the pages. Adding related images on subcategories also helps the website become visually more attractive. We could also optionally enable/disable a category at any time and decide the sort order of categories.

Have a go hero – adding more categories and subcategories

Now, add more categories and subcategories for the online shoe store. Try adding multiple level subcategories similar to a tree structure. Also play with the Sort Order field and see how it affects the appearance of categories.

 Hint: Women's **shoes** | **Boots** | **Platforms** categories

Have a go hero – deleting pre-installed images

Now, free your image manager by deleting pre-installed images. You can do this either by deleting each image one-by-one using image upload screens or by using cPanel file manager, or alternatively FTP to delete all image files in OpenCart system under images/data directory.

Adding manufacturers (brands)

We can provide more information about a product to visitors by defining manufacturers (brands). The brands data also will be listed under product detail page and interested users can click on a brand name to browse all listed items under this brand. For our Athletic men's shoes category, we can use sample brand names like Adidas, Reebok, Puma, and so on.

Time for action – adding Reebok as shoe brand

We will now see how to add Reebok as a shoe brand on our store.

1. Browse the **Catalog | Manufacturer** menu in the administration panel and click on the **Insert** button.

2. Write **Reebok** as **Manufacturer name** and select the default store name from the available **Stores** list. Then, we can provide the Reebok logo as an image in a similar way as we did for categories previously. Finally, click on the **Save** button to finish.

What just happened?

We have finished adding a sample brand name for our store. It is a common practice to provide company logos as an image in many real online stores. This way, our store would also look more attractive and informative.

Have a go hero – adding more sample brands

Now, add Puma and Adidas as other brands for the shoe store.

Adding products

Adding a product for online store involves several steps. OpenCart product definition interface is very easy to use, and well planned in tabs to take the required data in groups.

Time for action – adding a Reebok shoe model as a product

We will add a Reebok shoe model and assign it to Athletic sub-category under Men's shoes. We will also define all the basic data for the shoe model including price, main image, brand info, stock information, etc.

1. Open the **Catalog | Products** menu and click on the **Insert** button.

2. We have to give a **Product Name** for our shoe model at first. Then, we can optionally provide **meta tag description** and **description,** which will appear on the shoe details page. Let's write **Reebok Fuego Running Shoe** for the product name. Then, click on the **Data** tab to continue.

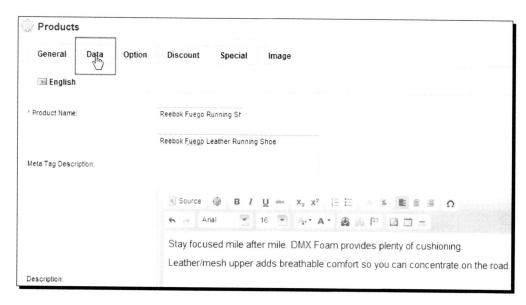

3. We have to write a uniquely defined product for the mandatory **Model** field. We can write **item no** as the model value, as shown in the following screenshot. We can optionally provide SKU for the product.

Basically, **SKU (Stock Keeping Unit)** is a unique identifier for each distinct product and service that can be purchased. SKUs are often used to refer to different versions of the same product. For example, a retail store carrying Guitar Hero 3 might have six SKUs, two for each of the three platforms—one with and one without a guitar.

Read more about SKU on:

`http://en.wikipedia.org/wiki/Stock-keeping_unit`

4. Then, we should provide the main image for the shoe. We already know how to use Image Manager. So, let's upload a suitable image for the product. Let's choose Reebok from the manufacturer option. Since our product is a physical one, we choose **Requires Shipping** option as **Yes**.

> Note that downloadable products will not require shipping.

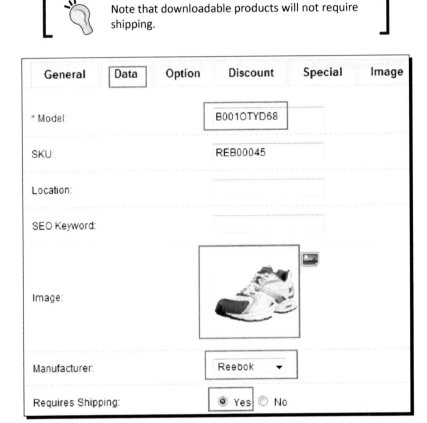

5. Let's give **20** for the **Quantity** in the stock for this shoe model. We should give a sales **Price**. In this example, we have provided **45**. Leave the other fields at their default settings for our example.

Optionally, we could change **Date Available** field which shows when the product will be enabled on the store. So, it is possible to define products which will be activated on a future date.

Out of Stock Status defines which message will be shown on product detail page to customers when the product goes out of stock. The default value is **2 - 3 days**. We could also show Out of Stock, In Stock, Pre-order values as a message as well.

By changing **Status** field, we are able to enable/disable a product from sitewide visibility.

We will talk about **Tax Class** in next chapter.

We could also provide more physical information about the product using the **Length**, **Weight**, **Dimensions** fields. This could be important for certain types of products. For example, with a marble block for decoration, a customer would certainly need to know about dimensions.

Notice that we didn't provide a currency ($, Euro, and so on.) for the price. We will return to this topic in later chapters.

6. We will choose the **Men's shoes > Athletic** subcategory for this product. Just because we currently have one store, we will select it from the **Stores** list. Since it is our first product, we can't choose any **Related Products** yet.

> The Related Products section helps visitors to browse for similar items on the product details page.

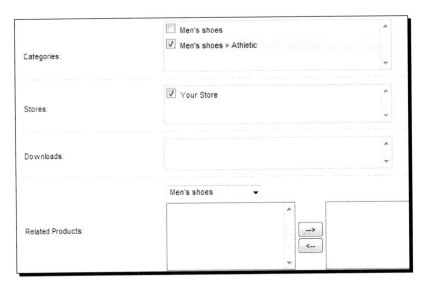

7. We will ignore the other tabs for now since we will review them later. Let's click on the **Save** button to complete a basic product; in this specific case, an athletic men's shoe model for our online shoe store.

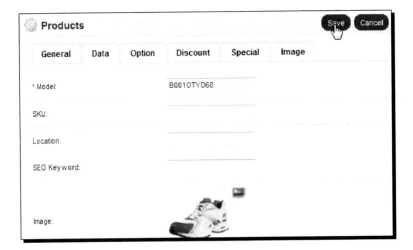

8. We now see the added shoe model in the products listings.

9. Let's browse into our shop interface and find the newly added shoe. As you can see from the screenshot, it is available for purchase:

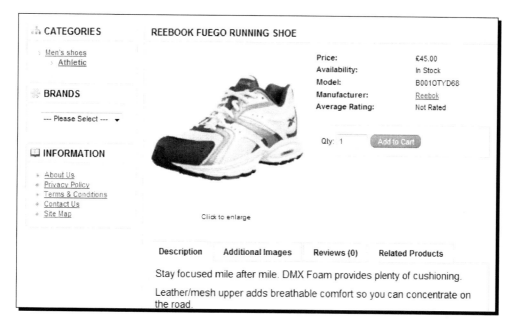

What just happened?

We have defined a shoe model with the minimum essential data. Notice that we have just left some options on their default settings. We will talk about them later.

Notice that online store visitors can buy this shoe model, but they are not able to choose a color or a size. Without these purchase options, the store would not operate professionally.

Time for action – adding purchase options for customers

Now, let's learn how we can define different color purchase options for our Reebok Fuego shoe model.

1. Browse to **Catalog|Products** listings and click on the **Edit** button near the listed shoe model.

2. Let's open the **Option** tab and click on the **Add Option** button. As soon as we do this, a new section will appear under this button. We write **Color** for the **Option** field. Finally, let's click on the **Add Option Value** button.

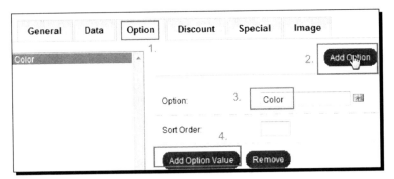

3. A new section will be added under the **Color** option. Now we can add different color options. Let's add **Black** for **Option Value** and define that we have **10** of them in the stock by filling the **Quantity** field. As the shoes with the black color option are sold, the total stock amount will be decreased accordingly, since we have chosen **Subtract Stock** field as **Yes** by default. Then, let's click on the **Color** option in the list on the left-hand side.

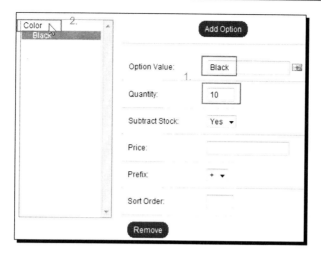

4. Let's define another color option, **Blue**, similar to the previous one. Finally, let's add a **Special Design** option value. Note that for the last option value, we have filled the **Price** field as **15**. Notice the **+** in the **Prefix** field. Its purpose is to add this price to base price of the product if this option value is selected. So, if the Black shoe is sold for 45, the Special Design shoe will be sold for 45 + 15 = 60. This is the power of option values.

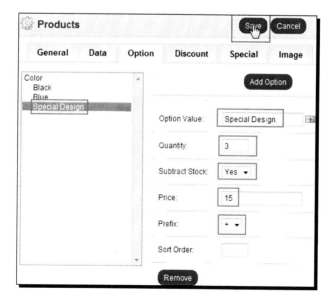

Notice that we can remove any **Option** or **Option Value** using the **Remove** button. Let's click on the **Save** button to complete adding the **Color** option with three option values (**Black, Blue, Special Design**).

5. Let's open the product details for this shoe again. Notice that we now **Color** in the **Available Options** list. Visitors had to choose one from the listed section. The **Black** color was selected by default because it is the first option we had added.

 We could use Sort Order to arrange orders of the options and option values.

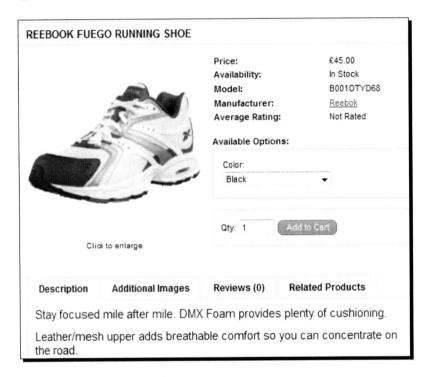

REEBOOK FUEGO RUNNING SHOE

Price:	£45.00
Availability:	In Stock
Model:	B001OTYD68
Manufacturer:	Reebok
Average Rating:	Not Rated

Available Options:

Color:
Black ▼

Qty: 1   Add to Cart

Click to enlarge

Description   Additional Images   Reviews (0)   Related Products

Stay focused mile after mile. DMX Foam provides plenty of cushioning.

Leather/mesh upper adds breathable comfort so you can concentrate on the road.

6. Let's choose the **Special Design** option from the list and click on the **Add to Cart** button.

Available Options:

Color:
Special Design +£15.00 ▼

Qty: 1   Add to Cart

7. As you can see from the updated shopping cart, the final sub-total price for the shoe has increased to **60** because of additional +15 price coming from Special Design option. The shopping cart also put **Color Special Design** as a note under the product name in a format of Option + Option value.

What just happened?

We have learnt how to add more features to a product by using options and option values. This way, we can add as many features as we want for an item. The more such options we add, the more flexible customers will be to choose the item with the features they want.

Pop quiz – understanding option values

Suppose that we have a boots shoe model with anti-slippery feature by default. It is priced at 40. What should we do to sell the same boots shoe model without anti-slippery feature at 30.

1. We should add the same product twice, with the same photos, name them accordingly, and set the prices separately.

2. We should name the product as Boots Shoe Model with a price at 30. Then we should add thr Anti-Slippery feature as an option with +10 price.

Have a go hero – adding size option and its option values

A feature to select shoe size is essential for any online shoe store. So, it is now your turn to add a size option with several sample size option values, such as 8, 8.5, 9, and 9.5. Then, do not forget to browse the final shoe details page to see how it will look and check the added functionality for customers.

Time for action – adding additional images for Reebok shoe

The more images we add for a certain shoe, the better they help a customer to decide about their final buying decision.

1. Let's open the newly added shoe model in the **Products** listings page and browse to the **Image** tab. Then, let's click on the **Add Image** button.

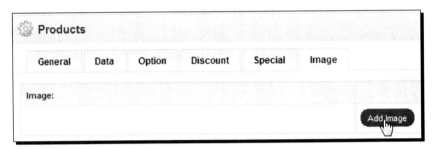

2. We can add as many images as we want by using the small icon. After adding some sample images, click on the **Save** button to complete this process.

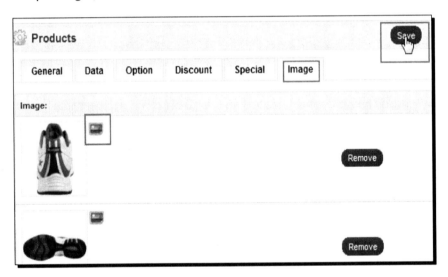

3. We can see the other images of the shoe when we browse to the item details page and click on the **Additional Images** tab.

What just happened?

We have seen how easy it is to add additional images for a product. Generally, it is a better experience for customers browsing more images on an online shoe store and it increases the overall quality of the store.

Summary

Categories and product definitions are the core elements of a store. Being careful about designing a category, subcategory structure, and providing as much information as we can in product definition screens, all increases the effectiveness of an online store. If you have difficulties in organizing your store, just browse the Internet for similarly themed stores. This way you can get the base category structure and further customize according to your needs.

In this chapter, we learned how to organize categories and add categories, products. We have seen using the product options will positively affect customer browsing experience.

In the next chapter, we will learn about Tax Management, another essential part of an online store which affects the overall pricing policy of the store.

3
Tax Management

In most cases, the tax rate for an online order was simply calculated according to shipping location. OpenCart has an easy to use, simplified tax system which works according to geographic zones of customer shipping addresses.

In this chapter we shall learn about:

◆ The basics of taxes according to shipping address

◆ Types of OpenCart Geo Zones

◆ Adding a Geo Zone

◆ Assigning a Geo Zone to a tax class

◆ Assigning a tax class to a product

◆ Displaying prices without tax on storefront

◆ How checkout pages change the final price according to different tax classes

OpenCart tax system

OpenCart currently only supports defining tax rates according to the shipping address.

 For this section, we will ignore taxes which can be applied specifically on the customer type (retail, business, and so on), product type (clothing, food, and so on), total order weight, and so on.

Let's assume that our online store is located in the UK (so, most of the customers are from the UK) and the store ships items to selected EU (European Union) addresses including the UK, Germany, Spain, France, and Italy.

The following is a typical tax scenario for our shoe store (**excluding shipping prices**):

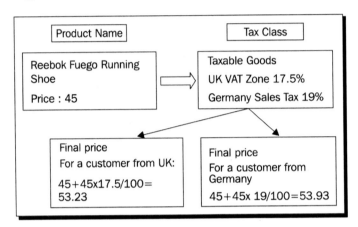

Understanding Geo Zones

Geo Zones represent the groups of countries or smaller geo sections under these countries. A Geo Zone can include countries, states, cities, and regions depending on the type of country.

OpenCart uses Geo Zones to identify **shipping** and **tax rate** price regulations for a customer's order.

Here is an example:

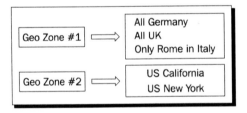

In this chapter, we will solely need Geo Zones for tax calculations.

Time for action – adding Germany as a Geo Zone for taxes

In this section, we will add Germany as a Geo Zone for our store to be used in tax calculations. We will include all regions under Germany.

1. Let's log in to the administration panel and click on the **System|Localisation|Geo Zones** menu item, as shown in the following screenshot. The administration panel is available at `http://yourwebsite.com/store/admin`.

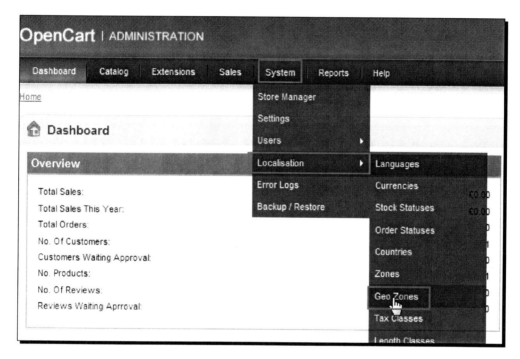

2. The page will list the Geo Zone names that were added upon installation. Let's click on the **Insert** button.

3. Let's write **Germany Tax Zone** for the **Geo Zone Name** field. Next, let's write **Germany Sales Tax Zone** for the **Description** field. Then, we will click on the **Add Geo Zone** button.

4. We will select **Germany** and **All Zones** under it. Then, we click on the **Save** button to finish adding Germany as a Geo Tax Zone.

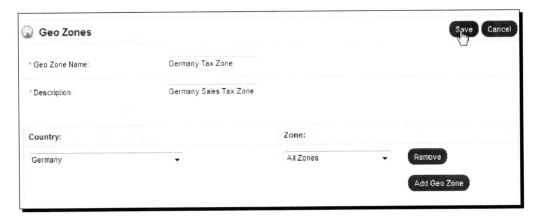

What just happened?

We have just finished adding Germany as a Geo Zone for taxes.

 We could select only a few regions from Germany if needed. Additionally, if we want to edit any Country and / or Zone definition in Geo Zones, we should visit System | Localisation | Zones menu in the administration panel.

Have a go hero – adding Rome, Milano / Italy as Geo Zone for taxes

Suppose that we only ship shoes to Rome and Milano in Italy and need to apply taxes for these regions. Define a new Geo Zone for these regions.

Tax classes

Tax classes include Geo Zones and they are connected to individual product items. A tax class can include more than one Geo Zone. You can think of a tax class as a connector between products and Geo Zones.

Time for action – adding the Germany Geo Zone to the default tax class

In this section, we will add the Germany Geo Zone to the default tax class and will apply its tax rate price.

1. Let's open the **System | Localisation | Tax Classes** menu.

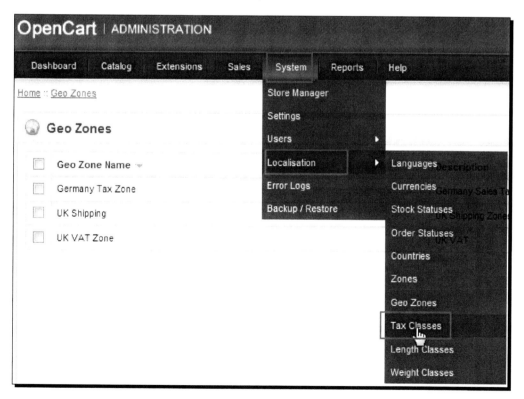

2. **Taxable Goods** tax class was listed. It was automatically created upon installation. Let's click on the **Edit** link.

3. As you can see from the following screenshot, this tax class includes **UK VAT Zone** by default in Geo Zone listings with a tax rate of **17.5%**. Let's click on the **Add Tax Rate** button.

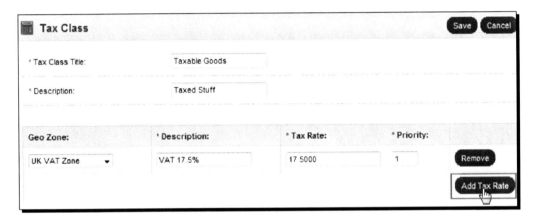

4. We select **Germany Tax Zone** from the available **Geo Zone** options. Let's write **Sales Tax 19%** for Description. We give **19** for Tax Rate. Finally, let's click on the **Save** button.

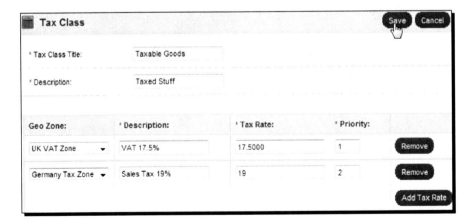

What just happened?

We already had a default tax class. It already included tax price for the UK Geo Zone. We have added the Germany Geo Zone as well and set its tax rate price.

Have a go hero – adding the Rome Milano Geo Zone to a new tax class

Now, it is your turn to add the Rome Milano Geo Zone to a new, separate tax class. Create a new tax class instead of using the default one.

Time for action – setting the tax class for a Reebok shoe

We will now see how setting a tax class for a product affects the overall price.

1. First, let's browse to the shoe example, which we added in the previous chapter, on storefront. Notice that the price is exactly the same as we had set in the administration panel in the previous chapter.

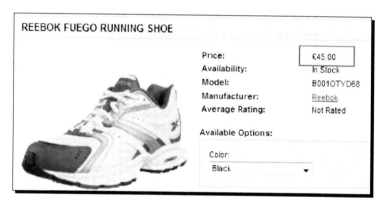

2. Let's open the administration panel and choose the **Catalog | Products** menu.

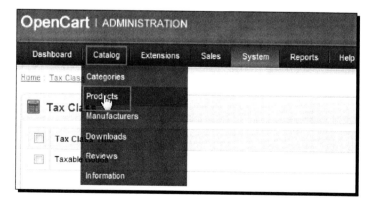

3. Let's **Edit** the shoe item on our store.

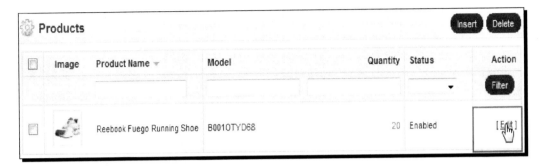

4. We browse to the **Data** tab, find, and change the **Tax Class** property to the
    Taxable Goods option. Do not forget to **Save** the changes.

5. We again browse to the shoe on the storefront and see that the price of the shoe has changed. The price increase is exactly the percentage of UK VAT rate, which was defined as 17.5%.

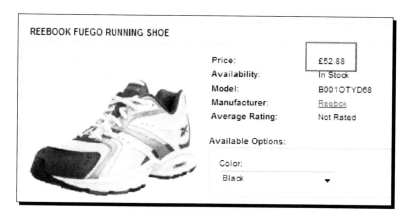

Now, carefully read the following section to understand why the UK VAT rate was applied automatically for this product even though there is also a Germany Sales Tax in this tax class.

What just happened?

An OpenCart store is installed by default according to the local settings for the United Kingdom and the products are shown on the online store with the inclusion of tax rate by default. This can be confusing for an international visitor. For example, a potential customer from Germany would see **taxed UK price** on the item properties page by default, which is a bad e-business practice.

On the other hand, remember that some specific countries can forbid showing prices without taxes for the customer. In this case, we have to show the tax value as well.

In a normal situation, we should better show the price of an item **without tax rate** on item pages and include the calculated tax rate on the final checkout screen.

Time for action – displaying prices without tax

We will now learn how to exclude tax prices from display on product pages.

1. Open the **System | Settings** menu.

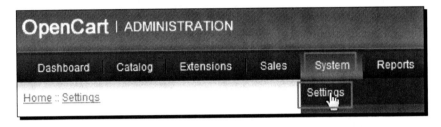

2. Let's open the **Options** tab.

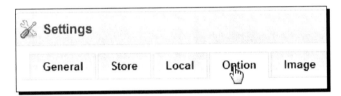

3. Notice the default **Option** settings for the store. We will select **No** for the **Display Prices with Tax** property. Then, let's click on the **Save** button.

4. We browse to the shoe information page and see that the price was set to **without calculated tax rate.**

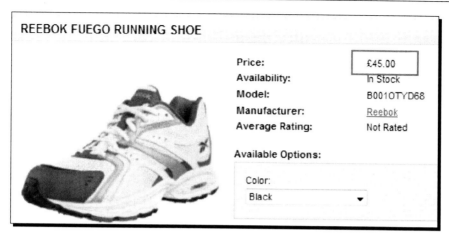

5. A customer from **Germany** will see the corresponding **Sales Tax 19%** value only on the final checkout page. This is shown in the following screenshot:

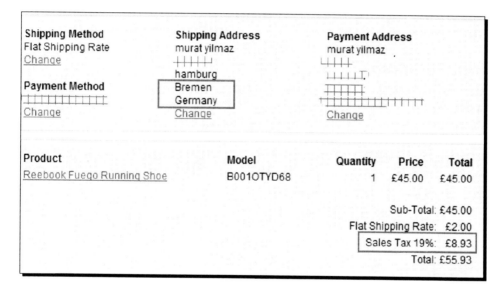

 You can test this by registering a customer and setting the shipping address to somewhere in Germany.

6. On the other hand, a customer from **United Kingdom** will see another tax rate, which is valid for UK shipping addresses, UK **VAT 17.5%**.

Shipping Method	Shipping Address	Payment Address
Flat Shipping Rate	murat yilmaz	murat yilmaz
Change		
	Cambridge	
Payment Method	Cambridgeshire	
Cash On Delivery	United Kingdom	
Change	Change	Change

Product	Model	Quantity	Price	Total
Reebook Fuego Running Shoe	B001OTYD68	1	£45.00	£45.00

Sub-Total: £45.00
Flat Shipping Rate: £2.00
VAT 17.5%: £8.23
Total: £55.23

What just happened?

We have changed **Display Prices with Tax** to **No** in our store settings. Using this method, all customers see the same price on product pages before going to checkout pages. They see the applied tax values only on checkout pages according to shipping address.

Pop quiz – understanding OpenCart taxes

Which of the following statements are true?

1. Each product can have more than one tax class in OpenCart.
2. We have to define a separate tax class for every Geo Zone we need.
3. Every product has to be assigned at least one tax class.

Summary

In this chapter, we have learned an essential part of an online store, tax management. Taxes directly affect the checkout price of a product. We have seen that OpenCart has a simplified tax management system that is based upon shipping address.

In the next chapter, we will learn how to configure store settings and customize according to our layout needs.

4
Configuring Store Settings

Upon installation, a store was created with a default design and store settings. We need to change several settings for the store; it is especially important to change the store name, description, store logo, and welcome message. The store is not SEO optimized by default. We will need to change this as well.

In this chapter we shall learn:

- Configuring General Store Information
- Activating SEO support
- Applying SEO for product pages
- Applying SEO for categories
- Installing OpenCart templates
- Activating OpenCart Module
- Using Google Talk module for online help
- Setting Information module for Privacy Policy, Terms and Conditions, etc.

General Store Information

General Store Information settings include store name, logo, welcome message, default currency settings, stock behavior options, several checkout, and price display options.

Time for action – configuring General Store Information

In this section, we will learn how to configure the most essential general store information.

1. Let's open the **System | Settings** menu. The **General** tab will be opened automatically and we will be able to provide essential general store information for our default store. We will fill the **Store Name**, **Store Owner**, **Address**, **Email,** and **Telephone** fields. **Store URL** is automatically filled in. We don't need to make changes on it.

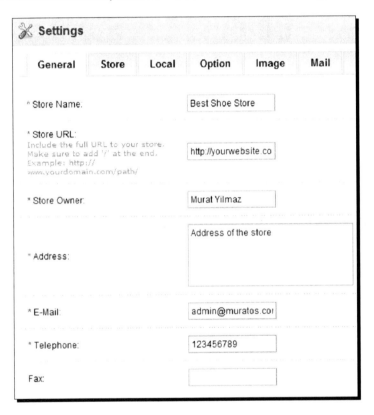

2. We will now open the **Store** tab where we will fill **Title**, **Meta Tag Description** fields, lets not ignore these fields. These are included in HTML head section and help to improve on-site SEO. The single default template for the store is selected. We don't need to touch this section.

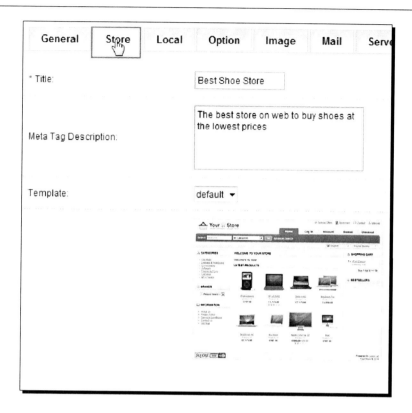

We will see **Welcome Message** section when we scroll down on the same tab page. We should certainly fill it.

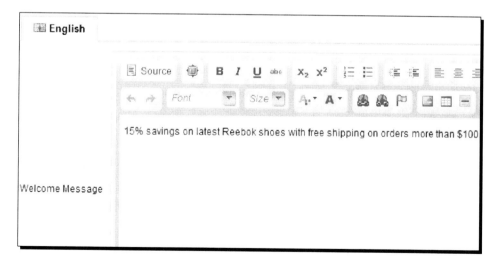

The welcome message is shown on the storefront, on the center, as shown in the following screenshot:

 The welcome message field is a perfect place to inform visitors about the latest promotions and news about the store, as we can even use very advanced HTML designs here with images.

3. The **Local** tab determines how our site will behave for store visitors **by default**. We assumed that our store is **California** based and because of this, we changed **Currency** to **US Dollar**. We can choose the default **Language** for the store. Here, **English** is selected by default for both the storefront and administration panel. The **Auto Update Currency** option should be set to **Yes** if we have defined more than one currency. The values are retrieved from Yahoo Finance automatically each day.

4. Let's continue with the **Option** tab. We want to show prices without tax value added on product pages. So, we have chosen to set the **Display Prices with Tax** option to **No**. This way, the final prices will be shown only on checkout pages.

 Please refer to Chapter 3, *Tax Management* for tax details.

We have left **Customer Group** field in **Default** setting.

 This is discussed in Chapter 9, *Managing Customers and Users* in detail.

It is logical to show prices all the time, not depending on whether a visitor has made a login or not. So, we have chosen **No** for the **Login Display Prices** feature. We preferred to automatically **Approve New Customers** by choosing **No**. This way, interested customers can buy immediately after registration without waiting. Finally, we have allowed **Guest Checkout** by choosing **No**. Some customers prefer to be able to shop without any registration process, immediately.

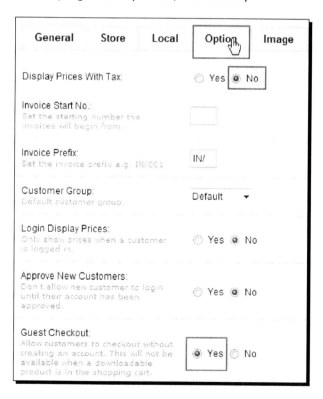

5. For legal safety purposes, it is advised to show **Privacy Policy** and **Terms & Conditions** terms in account registration and before completing the checkout. It is a common practice on most professional online stores. The positive side is that no one actually reads them!

6. There are several Stock options we can set for a store. It is a common practice to not show the **Display Stock** quantity. We will show **Out of Stock** if the product is out of stock but also added **Stock Status**, stating that it will be available in **2-3 Days** as default. It is advised to review an order before setting it to Completed status. So, when an order is processed, it will be set to **Pending** for our final review. If we want to track inventory, we would also use the **Stock Subtract** option.

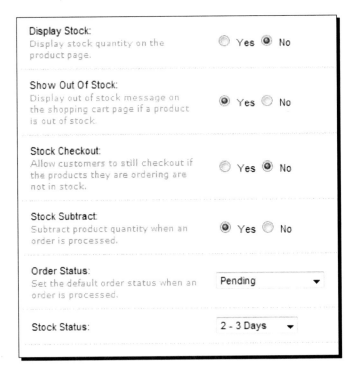

7. The final tab is **Image**. We can change our **Store Logo** and use an **Icon** for web browsers. All uploaded images are automatically resized according to the following settings. So, we can change them according to our needs. Finally, do not forget to click on **Save** button. Please, remember that the **Save** button saves all the information on all tabs. If you forget it, you will lose all changes in all tabs.

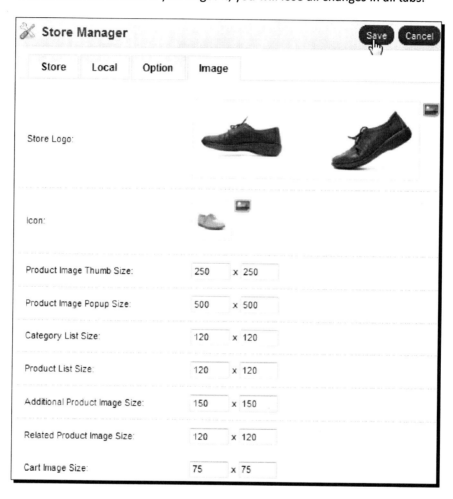

8. This is how our store will look after setting several general store options:

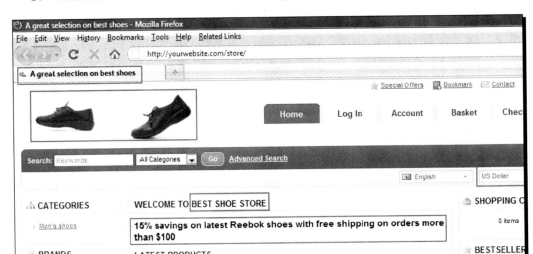

What just happened?

We have just finished changing several general store settings. These included changing store name, logo, welcome message, default currency settings. Then we have changed several stock, price display, and checkout options. Finally, we have checked the main store page to see how these changes affected the overall look.

Have a go hero – testing store configuration settings

Now, register as a test customer to your store. Test every item in the **Store Manager |
Option** tab to see how it will affect the customer experience by making sample orders. For example, Display Stock, Default Order Status, Subtract Stock, Showing Account Terms, etc.

OpenCart and SEO

SEO (**Search Engine Optimization**) is a group of processes which is applied for websites to increase their visibility in search engine results to get more qualified traffic. For an online store, it is very important to apply at least the basic SEO techniques.

OpenCart system allows to provide a **SEO URL** for products with a keyword and inserts **Title** and **Description Meta tags** in HTML source of these pages. These are the minimum requirements for optimized SEO for most search engines.

For using SEO URL, we would require that our hosting solution has installed `mod_rewrite` Apache module and allowed us to change `.htaccess` file.

There is plenty of free information about **SEO** and **SEO methods** in Google. Just doing a search on these keywords will bring many useful sources.

Here are a few useful blogs about SEO:

`http://www.seomoz.org/blog`

`http://www.seobook.com/blog`

Time for action – applying SEO for product pages

In this section, we will learn how to activate SEO URLs and apply to products.

1. Let's first browse to the product page and see how URL looks like before applying the SEO.

   Notice that the default URL before SEO is parametric and this is not good for search engine crawlers.

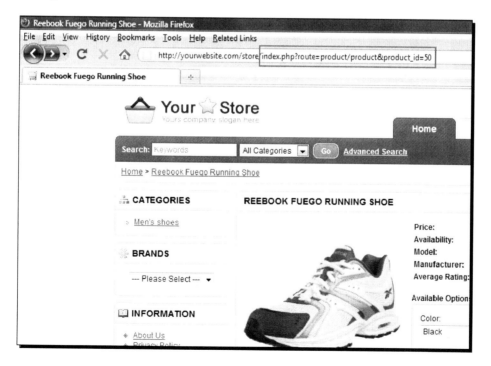

2. Let's login to the administration panel and open the **System | Settings** menu.

3. We will jump to the **Server** tab and choose **Yes** for the **Use SEO URLs** option. Then, let's click on the **Save** button.

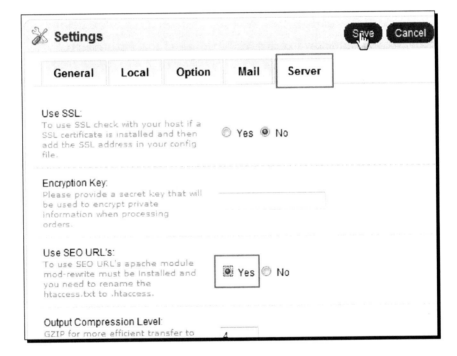

4. We will need to open cPanel and choose **File Manager** now.

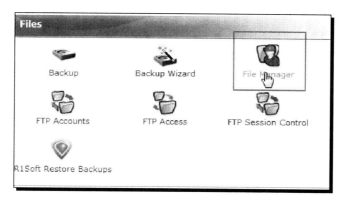

5. Let's open the root folder of our store and choose the **.htaccess.txt** file there. Right-click on it and choose **Rename**.

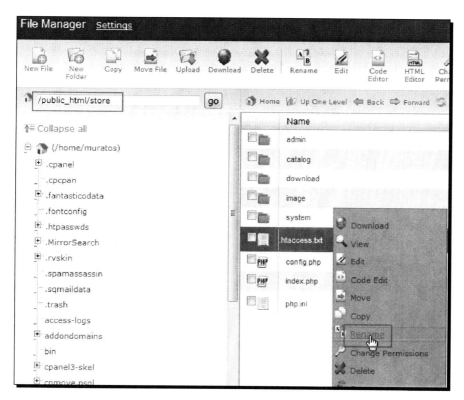

6. We will delete the .txt prefix. Thus, we will write **.htaccess** for the final filename. Then, click on the **Rename file** button.

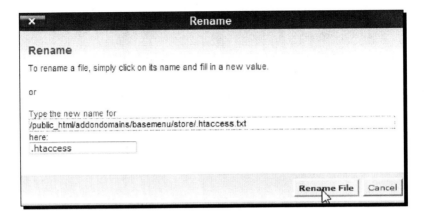

7. Let's return to the administration panel of our store and open the **Catalog | Products** tab.

8. Let's be sure that we have a nice, descriptive sentence(s) for **Meta Tag Description**. Most search engines take the first 160 characters of this field and show them in search engine results under the link to the page.

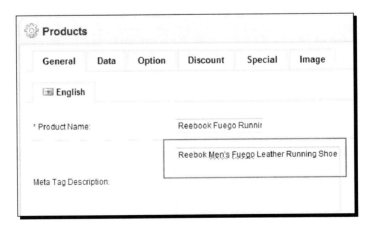

9. Let's open the **Data** tab. We should only change the **SEO Keyword** field. Notice that we have used – sign between the words of the key phrase. Click on the **Save** button to finish.

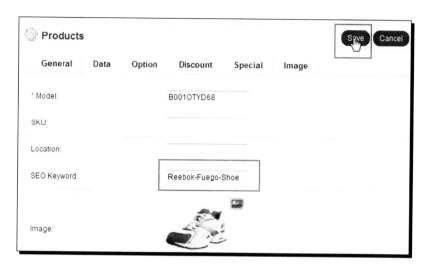

10. Let's browse to the product page and see how URL was changed according to SEO.

 If you get an error displaying the page, you should apply the next step as well. If you see that the page is correctly shown, the SEO exercise is finished here.

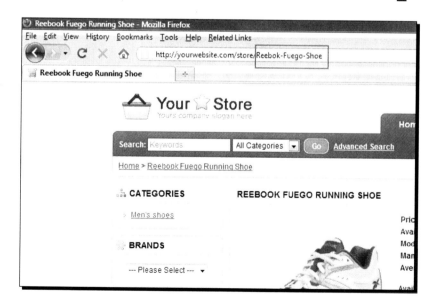

11. Let's open the **cPanel | File** manager again and the **Code Edit .htaccess** file.

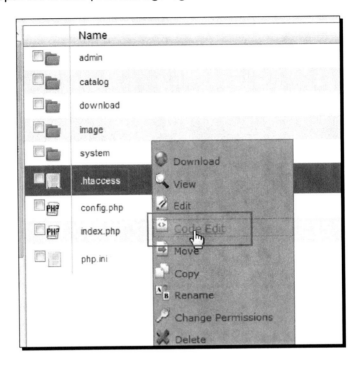

12. Just put a **#** sign in front of the **RewriteBase /** line. It will disable this line by commenting. Click on the **Save Changes** button.

```
# 1.To use URL Alias you need to be running apache with mod_rewrite enabled.
# 2. In your opencart directory rename htaccess.txt to .htaccess.
# For any support issues please visit: http://www.opencart.com

Options +FollowSymlinks

RewriteEngine On
# RewriteBase /
RewriteCond %{REQUEST_FILENAME} !-f
RewriteCond %{REQUEST_FILENAME} !-d
RewriteRule ^(.*)\?*$ index.php?_route_=$1 [L,QSA]
```

Open   Save Changes

An alternative option is to include path information if we have installed OpenCart on a directory rather than root. In the following example, the installation path is /store directory:

```
Options +FollowSymlinks

RewriteEngine On
RewriteBase /store
RewriteCond %{REQUEST_FILENAME} !-f
RewriteCond %{REQUEST_FILENAME} !-d
RewriteRule ^(.*)\?*$ index.php?_route_=$1 [L,QSA]
```

13. Browse to the page again. You should see that the page is correctly displayed. Open the HTML source in your browser. Notice the following SEO tags are correctly set:

```
<?xml version="1.0" encoding="UTF-8"?>
<!DOCTYPE html PUBLIC "-//W3C//DTD XHTML 1.0 Strict//EN" "http://www.w3.org/TR
<html xmlns="http://www.w3.org/1999/xhtml" dir="ltr" lang="en" xml:lang="en">
<head>
<title>Reebok Fuego Running Shoe</title>
<meta name="description" content="Reebok Men's Fuego Leather Running Shoe" />
<base href="http://basemenu.com/store/" />
<link href="http://basemenu.com/store/Reebok-Fuego-Shoe" rel="canonical" />
<link href="http://basemenu.com/store/image/data/cart.png" rel="icon" />
<link rel="stylesheet" type="text/css" href="catalog/view/theme/default/styles
```

What just happened?

We have learned how to activate the SEO option in settings. We then activated the .htaccess file. We have added a SEO Keyword for a product and finally checked how it looked, both in store front and in HTML source. We have learnt how to apply another change in the .htaccess file if we get an error.

Time for action – applying SEO for categories

In this section, we will learn how to apply SEO for categories. Categories are also well indexed by search engines. So, it is also advised to apply basic SEO for them.

1. Let's edit one of the categories. You can reach the category listings under the **Catalog | Categories** menu. Be sure to fill in **Meta Tag description**.

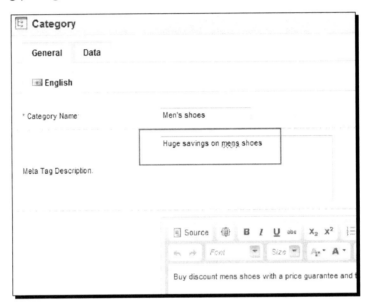

2. Let's open **Data** tab and fill in **SEO Keyword** field. Be sure to put – sign between words.

3. Here is how the SEO applied category URL will look:

What just happened?

We have learned how to apply SEO for a category.

> It is very important to **set a SEO Keyword for every category** in the store. For example, if we apply a SEO Keyword for a category and forget the subcategories under it, the category browsing may not be working correctly!

OpenCart and templates

Templates allow us to differentiate our store design. Some templates can also add new functionalities.

OpenCart has a very active developer and contributor community, which regularly releases new templates. There are both free and paid templates which we can use for our shop design. Here are some of the sources to find OpenCart templates according to the OpenCart version number which we use.

> Be sure that you backup your files before applying any templates and choose the right version.

Free templates from OpenCart website:

`http://www.opencart.com/index.php?route=extension/extension`

Paid OpenCart template websites:

`http://www.algozone.com/`

`http://www.opencarttemplates.com/store/`

`http://www.opencart-templates.com/`

`http://www.opencartstore.com/OpencartTemplates`

`http://theqdomain.com/ocstore/`

Time for action – installing an OpenCart template

In this section, we will learn how to upload an OpenCart template and activate it.

 Note that it shows the very basic template installation. Some complicated templates need to make changes on main store codes as well. These changes are generally explained step by step in a readme file in the template package.

1. The following screenshot shows that we have uploaded a template zip file to the **catalog/view/theme** folder in our store. We should **Extract** it to this folder.

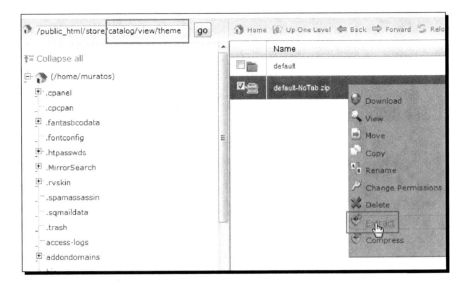

2. Let's just click on the **Extract File(s)** button.

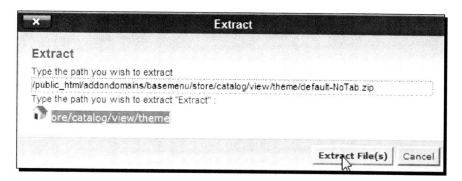

3. When we open **Store Manager** settings, we will now see that a new **Template** is listed. Let's choose it and **Save** the setting.

4. The following screenshot shows the main page after a new template was applied. Notice that there are only a few cosmetic changes to the design of the store.

What just happened?

We have just finished uploading and activating a basic template.

 We should not forget to backup our files beforehand if any code changes are required for templates in store codes.

OpenCart modules

In OpenCart, the left and right columns of the store are configurable by using modules.

The following screenshot shows the Categories, Brands, Information, Shopping Cart, and Bestsellers modules:

OpenCart is installed with a bunch of default modules. You can add other free or paid modules according to your needs.

 www.OpenCart.com contributions and forum pages are the essential sources to find new modules and/or ask for new ones from developers.

Time for action – installing Google Talk module for Online Help

In this section, we will learn how to install and activate the Google Talk module on the right-hand side. By using the Google Talk module on our store, the visitors can contact us at any time with any questions. It is a free and effective method of online help for a store.

1. Let's open the **Extensions | Modules** menu.

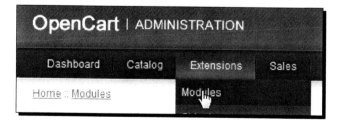

2. We see that many modules were installed by default. We will need to click on the **Install** button near the **Google Talk** line.

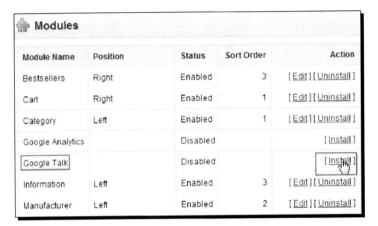

3. The Google Talk module was installed. Let's click on the **Edit** button for further settings.

4. We need to paste **Google Talk Code**, choose the **Position** of the module, and set the **Status** to **Enabled**. Do not forget to click on the **Save** button.

 You can get more information and install Google Talk software / browser plug-in on your computer here: `http://www.google.com/talk/`.

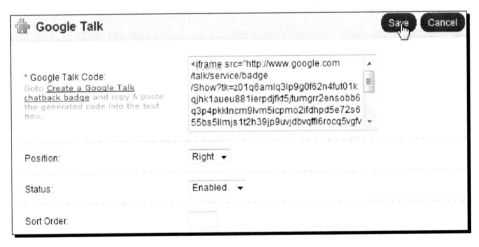

5. As you can see from the following screenshot, Google Talk is now enabled on the top right of our store as a module.

What just happened?

We have just activated the Google Talk module. Then, we inserted it on the top right of our store as an online help section.

Information module

The Information module provides essential information about the store which includes the About Us, Privacy Policy, and Terms and Conditions pages by default. We can update these pages and add new ones if we need other informative pages on OpenCart.

Time for action – updating Privacy Policy module information

In this section, we will learn where to update an Information module section, particularly Privacy Policy for our store.

1. Let's open the **Catalog | Information** menu.

2. Let's **Edit** the Privacy Policy line.

3. We can change **Information Title**, write a **Description**, and apply **SEO URL**. Let's click on the **Save** button to finish.

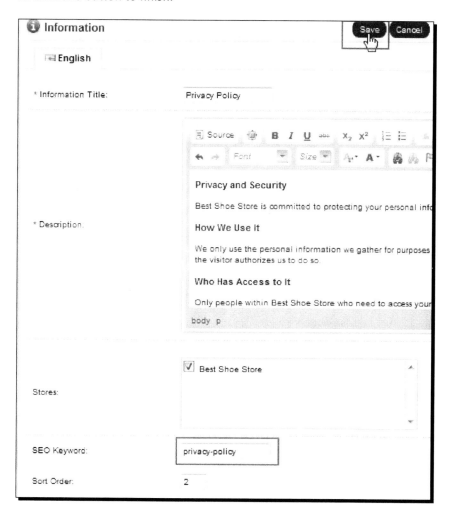

4. The following screenshot shows the updated **Privacy Policy** page:

What just happened?

We have learned how to change Privacy Policy for our store.

Pop quiz – understanding SEO for online stores

Which of the following statements are true?

a. We should immediately enable SEO URLs before submitting our store to search engine directories.

b. If we add a SEO keyword for a category, we certainly need to add keywords for other categories.

Running Multiple Stores in a Single Installation

OpenCart allows us running multiple stores in a single installation. Now, let's learn how we can achieve this.

Let's suppose that our first store is running at `http://yourwebsite.com/store` and we want to run the second store at `http://store2.yourwebsite.com`.

Here are the brief steps to start running the second store.

We should first define the **store2** subdomain using **cPanel** utility:

1. Open cPanel utility and browse to the Domain | SubDomain section.

2. We should fill **SubDomain** field as **store2** as our store will run on `http://store2.yourwebsite.com`.

3. We will need to change **Directory Root** field according to first running store's installation folder. In this case, it is `/public_html/store` folder.

4. Let's complete adding subdomain by clicking on the **Create** button.

The next part of setting up second store involves using **OpenCart Admin** panel:

1. Let's browse into **System | Settings** menu.

2. We click on **Create A New Store** button on the top.

3. We fill all the needed fields on all tabs to customize the second store with vital information like Welcome message, localization settings, etc. The most important setting is the Store URL field in which we should write `http://store2.yourwebsite.com`.

4. Let's click to **Save** to finish.

5. Now, we should assign individual products, categories by editing each of them.

Let's remember that we can only run multiple stores on different domains or subdomains. So, it would not be possible to run another store on another subfolder such as `http://yourwebsite.com/store2`.

Summary

In this chapter, we have learned how to change the basic store information. Customizing store settings and enabling SEO is top priority. Using the Welcome Screen effectively with a good template can also increase the overall quality of the store.

In the next chapter, we will continue by learning payment models which our store can accept. These will include PayPal, Cash on Delivery, Bank Transfer, and other popular payment gateways.

5
Setting Payment Models

Enabling a store to accept credit cards online and other alternative payment methods for customers is vital for high availability of an online store.

In this chapter we shall learn:

- The basics of online credit card processing
- Merchant account
- Payment gateway
- PayPal as a payment method
- The differences between several PayPal services
- Bank Transfer, Cheque or Money Order, Cash on Delivery payment options

We should clearly understand the three core elements of accepting credit card payments for an online store before starting on the details of online credit card processing.

Shopping cart system

The shopping cart is special software which allows customers to add / delete products to a basket from a store catalogue and then complete the order. The shopping cart also automatically updates the total amount which the customer will pay according to product additions or deletions on the basket.

OpenCart provides a built-in shopping cart system which provides all such functionality. So, you don't need to install or buy separate software for the shopping cart.

Merchant account

A merchant account is a special account type which differs from a usual bank account. Its sole purpose is to accept credit card payments. Opening a merchant account requires making a contract with the credit card network providers. Authorized card payments on the store are transferred to the merchant account. Then, as a merchant we can transfer the amount from merchant account to bank account (checking account).

Since opening a merchant account can be a tiresome process for most businesses and individuals, there are various online businesses which can provide this functionality. We will learn about them in the next section.

 Curious readers can learn the details of merchant accounts on the following links:

http://en.wikipedia.org/wiki/Merchant_account

http://www.merchantaccount.com/

Payment gateway

A payment gateway is an online analogue of a physical credit card processing terminal that we can locate in retail shops. Its function is to process credit card information and return the results back to the store system.

You can imagine the payment gateway as an element in the middle of an online store and credit card network. The software part of this service is included in OpenCart but we will have to use one of the payment gateway services, which we will briefly review in the next section.

Understanding online credit card processing

The following diagram shows the standard credit card processing flowchart in detail. Note that it is not essential to know every detail in steps shown in a red background color. These parts are executed on behalf of us by the payment system which we will use, so it is isolated both from the store and customer. For example, PayPal is such a system, which we will learn about now in detail.

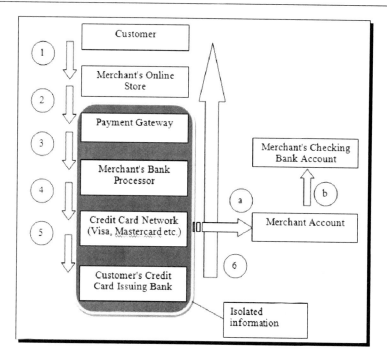

Let's explain the flowchart step by step to clearly understand the whole process:

1. A customer successfully enters into the checkout page after filling the shopping cart with the products. Then, he/she enters the credit card information and clicks on the **Pay** button.

2. Now, the store checkout page sends these details along with the total amount to the payment gateway securely.

3. The payment gateway starts a series of processes. First of all, the information is passed to the merchant's bank processor where the merchant account was opened before.

4. The information is then sent to the credit card network by this processor. Visa and MasterCard are two of the most popular credit card networks.

5. The credit card network processes the validity of the credit card and sends the information to the customer's credit card issuer bank.

6. As a result, the bank rejects or approves the transaction and sends the information back to the credit card network. Through the same routing in reverse, the payment information is finally submitted back to the online store with a special code. All this is done in a few seconds and the information flow starting from the payment gateway is isolated from both the customer and merchant. It means that we don't have to deal with what's going on after sending information to the payment gateway. As a merchant, we only need the result of the transaction.

After the information is processed by credit card network during Step 6; the transaction funds are transferred to the merchant account by the credit card network as shown in Step **a**. Then, the merchant can transfer the funds from the merchant account to the usual checking bank account automatically or manually, as shown in Step **b**.

OpenCart payment methods

The current OpenCart version supports many established payment systems, including PayPal services, Authorize.net, Moneybookers, 2Checkout, and so on, as well as basic payment options such as Cash on Delivery, Bank Transfer, Check/money order, etc.

 We can also get more payment gateway modules on the OpenCart extensions section by searching in Payment Methods.

`http://www.opencart.com/index.php?route=extension/`
`extension`

We will now briefly learn the most widely used methods and their differences and similarities to each other.

PayPal

PayPal is one of the most popular and easiest to use systems for accepting credit cards for an online store. PayPal has two major products to be used in OpenCart through built-in modules:

- PayPal Website Payment Standard
- PayPal Website Payment Pro

Both of these payment methods provide both payment gateway and merchant account functionality. Let's understand the details of each now.

PayPal Website Payment Standard

It is the easiest method to implement accepting credit card payments on an online store. For merchants, a simple bank account and a PayPal account is enough to take payments. There are no monthly fees or setup costs charged by PayPal. The only cost is a fixed small percentage taken by PayPal for each transaction. So, you should consider this on price valuations of items in the store.

Here is the link to learn about the latest commission rates per transaction:
`http://merchant.paypal.com`

When the customer clicks on the **checkout** button on OpenCart, he/she will be redirected to the PayPal site to continue with the payment.

As you can see from the following sample screenshot, a customer can provide credit card information instantly or log in to his/her PayPal account to pay from the balance in the PayPal account:

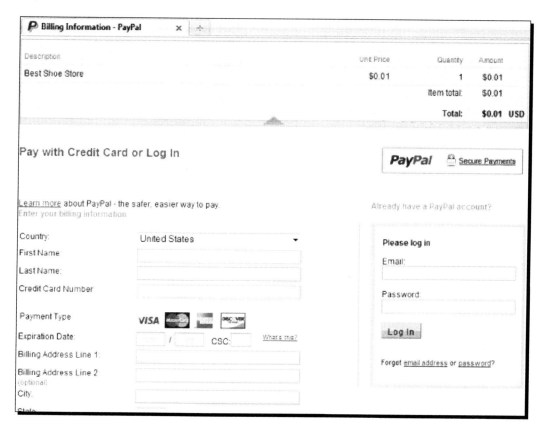

In the next step, after the final review, the user clicks on the **Pay Now** button.

Notice that PayPal automatically localizes the total amount according to the PayPal owner's account currency. In this case, the price is calculated according to Dollar – Euro exchange rates.

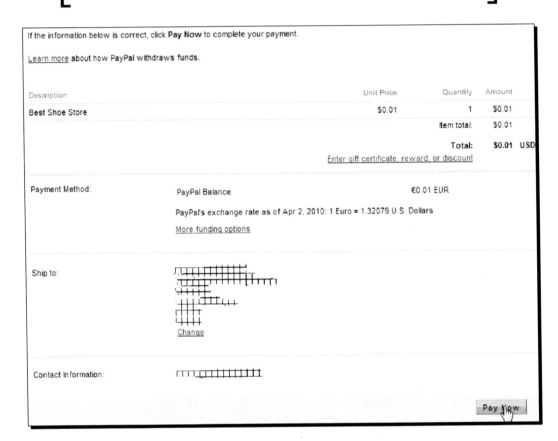

After the payment, the PayPal screen shows the result of the payment. The screen doesn't return to the merchant store automatically. There is a button for it: **Return to Merchant**.

Finally, the website user is informed about the result of the purchase in the OpenCart store.

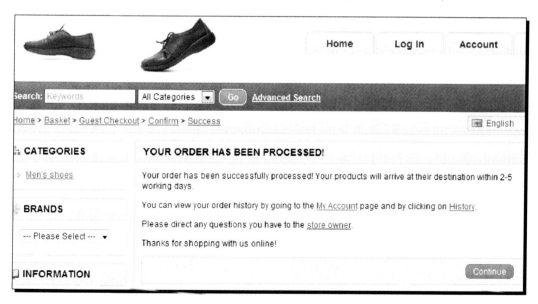

The main advantage of PayPal Website Payment Standard is that it is easy to implement; many online people are familiar with using it. We can state one minor disadvantage. Some people may abandon the purchase since the payment gateway would leave the store temporarily to complete the transaction on the PayPal website.

PayPal Website Payment Pro

This is the paid PayPal solution for an online store as a payment gateway and merchant account. The biggest difference from PayPal Website Payment Standard is that customers do not leave the website for credit card processing. The credit card information is completely processed in the online store as it is the popular method of all established e-commerce websites. Even the customers will not know about the processor of the cards. Unless we put a PayPal logo ourselves, this information is well encapsulated.

Using this method also only requires a bank account and PayPal account for the merchant. PayPal charges a monthly fee and a one-time setup fee for this service. The individual transactions are also commissioned by PayPal.

This is a very professional way of processing credit cards online for a store but it can have a negative effect on some customers. Some customers can require seeing some indication of trust from the store before making a purchase. So, depending the on store owner's choice, it would be wise to put a remark and logo of PayPal stating that **«Credit card is processed by PayPal safely and securely»**

For a beginner OpenCart administrator who wants to use PayPal for the online store, it is recommended to get experience with the free Standard payment option and then upgrade to the Pro option.

We can get more information on PayPal Website Payment Pro service at:

`http://merchant.paypal.com`

At time of writing this book, PayPal only charges a fixed monthly fee ($30) and commissions on each transaction. There are no other setup costs or hidden charges.

PayFlow Pro payment gateway

If we already have a merchant account, we don't need to pay extra for it by using PayPal Standard or PayPal Pro. PayFlow Pro is cheaper than other PayPal services and allows us to accept credit card payments to an existing merchant account.

> Unfortunately, OpenCart currently does not support it as a built-in module but there are both free and paid modules. You can get them from the OpenCart official contributions page at:
>
> `http://www.opencart.com/index.php?route=extension/`
> `extension`

Time for action – configuring PayPal Website Payment Standard

In this section, we will learn how to configure PayPal Website Payment Standard on OpenCart.

1. Let's open the **Extensions | Payments** menu in the administration panel.

2. We will find the **PayPal** line from the available payment method listings and click on the **Install** button.

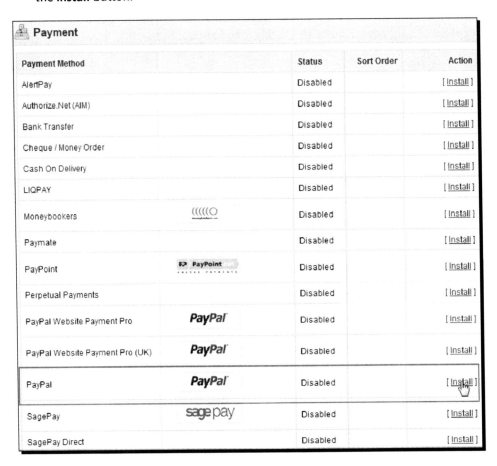

3. The next step is to **Edit** PayPal settings.

4. We provide our PayPal **E-Mail** address. Note that the payments will be made to this email address. So, be very careful to enter it correctly. We choose **Test Mode** as **No**.

We could select **Test Mode** as **Yes**. If we do this, the online store will send the transactions on the checkout page to virtual test accounts, which we set on the PayPal developer system beforehand. Actually, we do not need to set **Test Mode** to **Yes**. There is an easy way to test the system with real transactions, as we will learn about soon.

We set **Transaction Method** to **Sale**. As a common practice, we set **Order Status** to **Pending**. Since fraud payments are common, we will have a chance to look at the details of the payment and the order, before announcing to the customer that his or her order is complete.

Set **Geo Zone** to **All Zones** and **Status** to **Enabled**. Finally, let's click on the **Save** button.

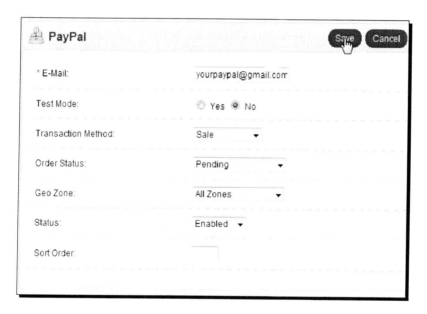

What just happened?

We have just finished enabling and setting up PayPal Standard Payment method. From now on, the customers can use PayPal or their credit cards to pay for the products online.

Have a go hero – testing PayPal Website Payment Standard method

Now, it is your turn to the test just-enabled PayPal Website Payment Standard method. All you need is to use another PayPal account with some balance on it and set some product prices as 0.01. This way, we can make tests on real PayPal transactions with small amounts. Register a customer and buy several products with this PayPal account on our store.

Time for action – configuring PayPal Website Payment Pro

In this section, we will learn how to configure PayPal Website Payment Pro on OpenCart.

 We already have a Website Payment Pro paid account to use this functionality. The details are at this link: `https://merchant.paypal.com/us/cgi-bin/?&cmd=_render-content&content_ID=merchant/wp_pro`.

1. First of all, we visit `http://www.paypal.com` and log in to the system. After this, let's click on the **Profile** link.

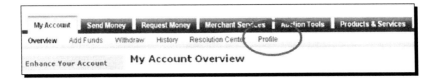

2. Let's click on the **API Access** menu.

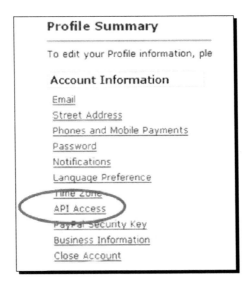

3. We will click on the **Request API Credentials** link.

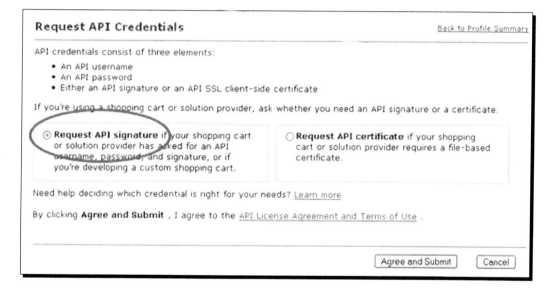

4. We will need to select the **Request API signature** option. Let's click on the **Agree and Submit** button.

5. The next page will list **API Username**, **API Password,** and **Signature**. Let's take a note of these values and click on the **Done** button to complete.

6. Let's open the **Extensions | Payments** menu in the administration panel.

7. Let's click on the **Install** link near the **PayPal Website Payment Pro** option.

8. We will edit the payment configuration details page. Let's provide the **API Username**, **API Password,** and **API Signature** values that we have retrieved from PayPal website in previous steps. We have the option to make operations on the Test server. Let's choose **No** for **Test Mode** to enable it on a real payment gateway. Let's choose **Transaction Mode** as **Sale**. We choose **Order Status** as **Pending** and **Status** as **Enabled**. This payment option will be available for **All Zones** according to current **Geo Zone** selection. Let's click on the **Save** button to complete the operation.

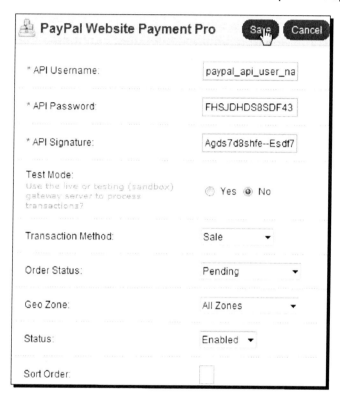

What just happened?

We have just finished enabling and setting the PayPal Website Payment Pro method. From now on, the customers can use their credit cards to pay for the products online without leaving the store for the payment process. All operations are done in store without any visible connection to PayPal.

 Readers who want to use PayPal Website Payments Pro UK version instead can go to the following link to open their business accounts and get API values:

```
https://www.paypal-business.co.uk/process-online-
payments-with-paypal/index.htm
```

Have a go hero – testing PayPal Website Payment Pro method

Now it is your turn to test just the enabled PayPal Website Payment Pro method. Make several test purchases with small 0.01 amounts on products. Be sure that all operations are completed in store without leaving to PayPal.

Authorize.net

This is a paid payment gateway service with similar functionality to PayPal Website Payment Pro. It means that customers can provide their credit card information without leaving the website and without any sign of `authorize.net` processing the information. So, this one is a paid service with an included payment gateway service and merchant account.

> Visit and compare the prices against the similar PayPal Website Payment Pro at www.authorize.net.
>
> We can also get more payment gateway modules on the OpenCart extensions section by searching in Payment Methods.
>
> `http://www.opencart.com/index.php?route=extension/`
> `extension`

Bank transfer

We can easily achieve being able to accept bank transfer payments by activating a module in OpenCart. The order of the customer is held in pending status until the bank payment is confirmed.

Time for action – accepting bank transfer on orders

In this section, we will learn how to enable the bank transfer module and use it.

1. Let's open the administration panel and click on the **Install** button near the **Bank Transfer** line.

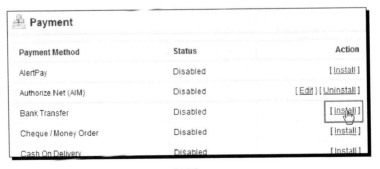

Payment Method	Status	Action
AlertPay	Disabled	[Install]
Authorize Net (AIM)	Disabled	[Edit] [Uninstall]
Bank Transfer	Disabled	[Install]
Cheque / Money Order	Disabled	[Install]
Cash On Delivery	Disabled	[Install]

2. Let's click on the **Edit** button.

| Bank Transfer | Disabled | [Edit] [Uninstall] |

3. We should provide our bank account information. The sample **Bank Transfer Instructions** are shown below. Set **Order Status** as **Pending** and **Status** as **Enabled**. Click on the **Save** button.

We could choose a specific **Geo Zone** to enable bank transfer solely for this zone. In our example, it is available to all customers worldwide. Notice that we can not have the same type but only separate payment options for different zones at the same time. It would require a third party module, which you can request or look for at the OpenCart extensions section.

```
http://www.opencart.com/index.php?route=extension/
extension
```

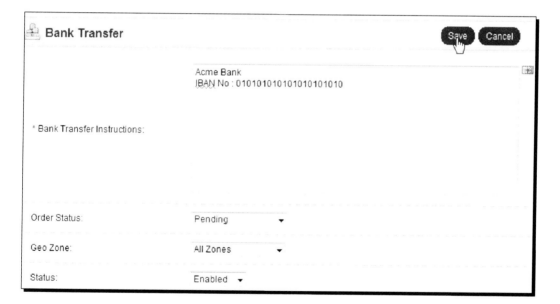

4. As you can see from the following screenshot, the Bank Transfer option will also be enabled on the checkout page as a payment method for the customer:

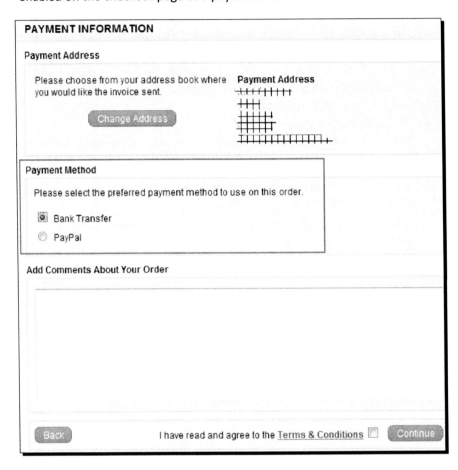

5. The following screenshot shows how the Bank Transfer Instructions we have provided will be shown before the customer confirms the order:

6. The following screenshot shows the order details on the administration panel. Notice that we had assigned **Status** as **Pending** by default:

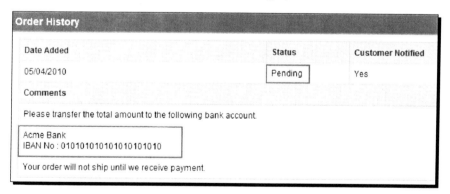

What just happened?

We have learned how to activate a bank transfer for our store. Then, we checked how it would look on checkout pages and in the order details screen in the administration panel.

Cheque / money order

With this payment option, we provide make cheque payable to information to the customer. The customer sends the cheque / money order to the store's default address by using this name. After we clear the check, order items are sent to the customer.

Cash on delivery

By using this option, the customer pays the money on delivery to the courier. We can use this option if we handle shipping with our own couriers. Some online stores also give the ability to customer to reject the order at the time of delivery. A common usage is with clothes and shoe stores. Customer tries the apparel and pays only for courier service if he/she doesn't like the product or it doesn't suit.

Have a go hero – activating cheque / money order and cash on delivery options

Now, it is your turn to enable check/money order and cash on delivery options. They are very similar to the bank transfer module and need similar fields.

Pop quiz – understanding online credit card processing

Which of the following statements are true?

1. PayPal does not provide a default merchant account. So, we have to open a merchant account before starting to use the PayPal Standard or Pro options.

2. To accept credit cards online, we have to make an agreement with a bank and/or credit networks such as Visa and Mastercard.

3. PayFlow Pro only provides payment gateway functionality. We should already have an opened merchant account before we start using it.

Summary

In this chapter, we have seen the essentials of online credit card processing and how a purchase is achieved as a result of complicated checks. Hopefully, we won't need to enter the details of credit card networks or merchant accounts. We have seen that payment gateways (with merchant account) like PayPal, `Authorize.net` can easily provide such solutions. We have seen how to enable PayPal and other basic payment methods for OpenCart.

In the next chapter, we will learn different shipping options and how to start using them.

6
Setting Shipping Methods

It is vital to provide the most affordable and high quality shipping service for customers. It is very common that many customers leave the checkout page just because the listed shipping method is very expensive. We should be careful that the sale price for items, plus shipping costs really cover our overall costs.

In this chapter we shall learn about:

- Limiting orders to certain countries
- Free shipping
- Flat rate shipping
- Per Item method
- Weight-based shipping
- UPS
- USPS

Accepting orders from certain countries

It is logical to eliminate client registrations completely from the countries where our store will never ship the items. For example, if our store only ships the items to US, Canada, and selected EU countries, we would need to disable other countries showing in OpenCart. OpenCart has all the countries of the world enabled by default on installation.

Time for action – shipping items to selected countries only

In this section, we will learn how to disable country and zone definitions from OpenCart to allow registrations from certain countries only. Let's assume that we will ship products only to US, Canada, UK, and Germany.

There are two methods to enable/disable the countries for shipping.

Manual method

1. Let's open the **System | Localisation | Countries** menu. We will **Edit** the first country, which we will disable.

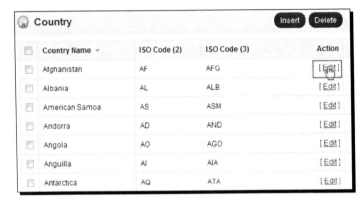

2. Let's choose **Country Status** as **Disabled**. Let's click on the **Save** button to finish.

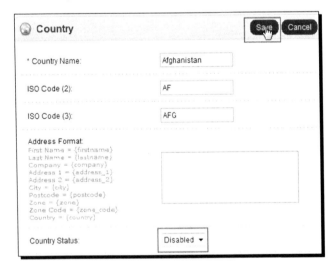

3. We should repeat this process for all pages of countries which we will not need, one by one. Note that it is a very time consuming process.

Automatic method

1. We will take advantage of phpMyAdmin database administration tool which we can reach at cPanel. Let's open cPanel which the hosting service has provided for us. Let's click on the **phpMyAdmin** link.

We should be very careful when applying operations on phpMyAdmin. A wrong operation can damage the whole store structure.

2. We list the content of the database and see the tables in our OpenCart installation. The information for countries is in the **country** table. Let's click on the **SQL** link on the top menu.

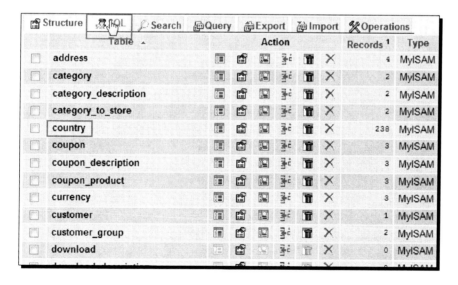

Table ▲	Action						Records [1]	Type
address							4	MyISAM
category							2	MyISAM
category_description							2	MyISAM
category_to_store							2	MyISAM
country							238	MyISAM
coupon							3	MyISAM
coupon_description							3	MyISAM
coupon_product							3	MyISAM
currency							3	MyISAM
customer							1	MyISAM
customer_group							2	MyISAM
download							0	MyISAM

3. Let's write the following SQL statement and click the **Go** button to execute it:

```
update country set status=0
```

This SQL query will disable all countries in the database.

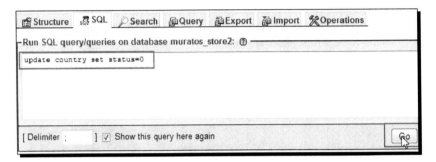

4. Now, it is easy to enable just a few countries one by one at the administration panel. For example, we would enable the US like in the following screenshot. We will repeat this for the remaining countries—Canada, UK, and Germany in this case.

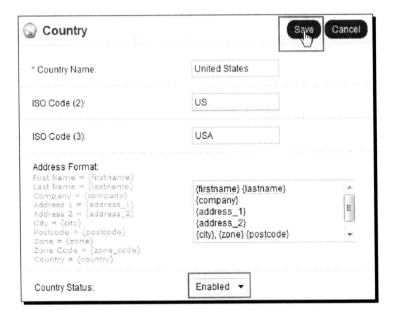

5. Now, if we try to register as a new customer, only enabled countries will be listed.

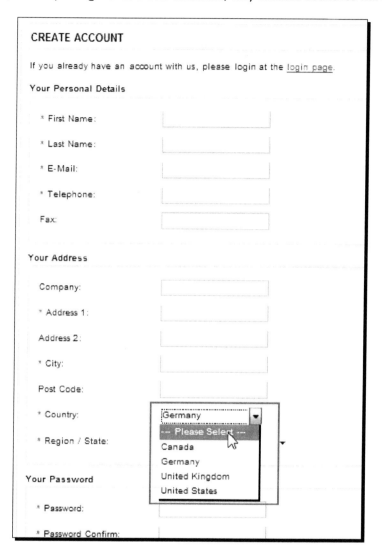

What just happened?

We have learned how to show a refined registration country listing for potential customers. Another alternative could be to also enable the countries which we plan to ship to in the future for registration. This way, we can retrieve the information of potential purchasers and send a newsletter stating that the store items are now shipped to their address.

For IT curious readers, here are the links for more information about phpMyAdmin and SQL queries.

`http://www.phpmyadmin.net`

`http://en.wikipedia.org/wiki/SQL`

Choosing a shipping method

The decision of which shipping method(s) we will use on our store is very important. OpenCart supports standard shipping methods including Free, Flat Rate, Per Item, and Weight Base Shipping and also enables us to use established shippers including UPS, USPS, and Royal Mail. We will cover the most important methods with examples.

Free shipping

In OpenCart, we can apply free shipping to an order. We can provide free shipping on all purchases without a minimum basket value or alternatively, a customer will see the free shipping option on the checkout page if his/her basket is bigger than our pre-defined value.

We should calculate the packing and shipping costs carefully before enabling free shipping since customers will not pay extra for it. Free shipping can be defined for all zones or only one zone. For example, free shipping for orders more than $200 for UK zone visitors.

Currently, free shipping cannot be applied on multiple zones separately on the default free shipping module. For example, free shipping on $200 for UK, $250 for Germany and so on.

Time for action – configuring free shipping for all UK customers with orders of more than $100

Suppose that our store resides in the UK and we want to apply free shipping if the total order value is more than $100, no matter how many products a customer purchases.

1. Let's open the **Extensions | Shipping** menu in the administration panel and click on the **Install** link near the **Free Shipping** item.

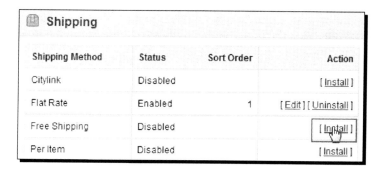

2. The next step is to **Edit** the free Shipping settings. Write **100** for **Total**, choose **Geo Zone** as **UK Shipping**, and **Status** as **Enabled**. Click on the **Save** button to enable **Free Shipping**.

3. In the following case, free shipping will be enabled since the customer shipping address is the UK and the order total is $180, which is bigger than the minimum free shipping condition of $100.

4. In the following case, the customer did not get the free shipping option even though he/she is from the UK. The reason is that the shopping cart value is less than $100.

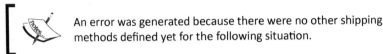

An error was generated because there were no other shipping methods defined yet for the following situation.

What just happened?

We have learned how to set up the free shipping method. Free shipping for orders more than a pre-defined value can encourage customers to buy more. Many established online stores use the free shipping method as a powerful tool for promotion and selling.

Flat rate shipping

Flat rate shipping is defined as when we don't want to deal with individual product or basket shipping rates. No matter the order amount, a fixed shipping charge is applied on it. As in the case of free shipping, it needs careful planning because some customers can order many products at once, leaving us with large shipping costs even though we only charge a flat rate for shipping. The common method is to secretly reflect the shipping and handling costs in each product price. Another alternative is to analyze sales and find the average order value and average shipping costs for the store. Then, a profitable flat rate shipping method is determined according to these values.

Time for action – configuring flat rate shipping for addresses in Germany

Let's apply $20 flat rate shipping for Germany addresses.

1. Flat rate shipping is enabled by default on installation. If it isn't enabled, let's open the **Extensions | Shipping** menu in the administration panel and click on the **Install** link near the **Flat Rate** item. Then, we will **Edit** the flat rate settings. Write **20** for **Cost**, choose **Tax Class** as **Taxable Goods**, **Geo Zone** as **Germany Tax Zone**, and **Status** as **Enabled**. Click on the **Save** button to enable **Flat Rate** shipping.

2. As you can see from the following screenshot, a customer from Germany will have a flat shipping rate of $20 no matter the amount of the shopping cart. A $20 charge is applied in the same way for a $10 or a $1,000 order.

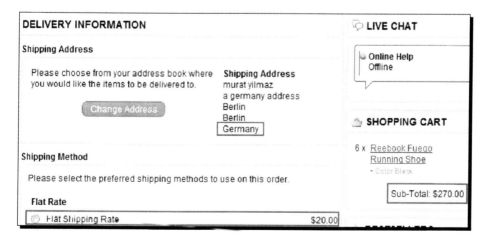

What just happened?

We have learned how to enable flat rate shipping for a certain zone. Remember that the flat rate shipping method value should be larger than average real shipping costs for the store.

Per item

When the per item method is applied, there is a shipping cost for each product in the basket. For example, if we apply a per item cost of $6, it would be $60 for 10 products in the basket no matter what the prices of the individual items. As in all shipping methods, it is possible to limit this shipping method on a Geo Zone.

Have a go hero – configuring per item method

Configuring the per item method is very similar to the flat rate method. Now, it is your turn. Define the per item cost as $6 for the US shipping zone and test the behavior on the client side by filling the shopping basket with several products.

Weight Based Shipping

Weight Based Shipping method applies to the overall weight of the order. The shipping cost is determined by ranges in OpenCart.

A sample calculation would be:

- If weight is smaller or equal to 1kg, shipping cost equals to $10
- If weight is between 1 kg and 2 kg, shipping cost equals to $17
- If weight is between 2 kg and 5 kg, shipping cost equals to $35
- If weight is more than 5kg, shipping cost equals to $60

Time for action – applying weight-based shipping method for US customers

In this section, we will learn how to enable weight-based shipping solely for US customers with sample weight—price ranges.

1. Let's open the **Extensions | Shipping** menu. After this, install and edit Weight Based Shipping method. A general tab will be opened. We should choose the **Enabled** option in the **Status** field. After this, let's click on the **US Shipping Zone** tab.

2. Let's fill the **Rates** according to the following screenshot. After this, we choose **Status** as **Enabled**. Let's click on the **Save** button to finish.

```
1:10.00,2:17.00,5:35.00,10:60.00
```

3. Let's edit a product on the store now. The products are under the **Catalog | Products** menu. We click on the **Data** tab on the product information page.

4. Let's scroll down the Data page until we find the **Weight** and **Weight Class** options. Change them according to the following screenshot:

5. Let's login to the storefront with a sample client with a US shipping address and create a basket with a weight of 1.50 kg. The Weight Based Shipping option for the US shipping zone with a value of $17.00 has appeared automatically, as shown in the following screenshot:

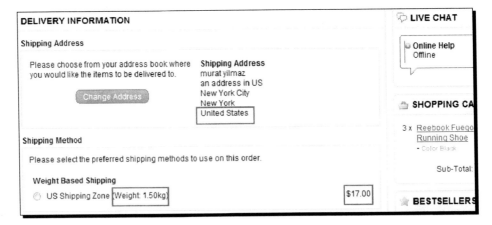

6. Now, let's increase the basket size to 3kg and check the page again.

What just happened?

We have enabled weight-based shipping for the US shipping zone with sample values. Let's understand the usage of rates clearly.

```
1:10.00,2:17.00,5:35.00,10:60.00
```

We should evaluate it like this: Up to 1 kg - $10; 1 to 2 kg - $17; 2 to 5 kg - $35 etc.

Pop quiz – Web Based Shipping Rates Usage

Suppose we are using `1:10.00, 2:17.00, 5:35.00, 10:60.00` as rates filed in Web Based Shipping method.

1. What would happen on the checkout page if the client has added items to the basket that weigh more than 10 kg?

2. Is it possible to enable web-based shipping for different zones at the same time?

UPS

UPS (**United Parcel Service**) is the world's largest package delivery company and we can take advantage of using the integrated UPS module of OpenCart. Before doing this, we will need to register at the UPS Developer Kit website to get the username, password, and an XML key for communication of OpenCart with UPS.

```
https://www.ups.com/upsdeveloperkit
```

Click on the Register link to start.

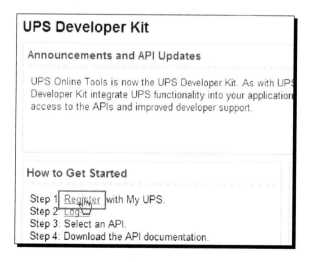

Complete your account details.

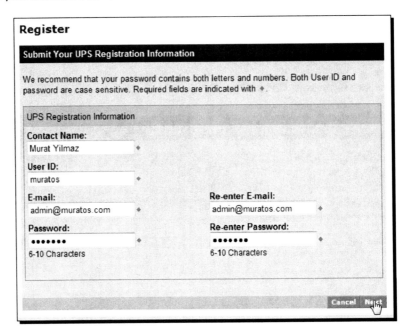

We will need to complete contact information, shipping defaults, email options, and payment defaults. The following screenshot shows how the beginning of the profile information page will look:

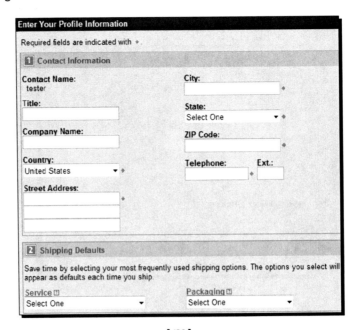

We haven't finished. Registering with the website is not enough. We should request an access key by applying online.

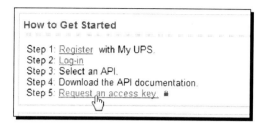

Note that this would require either opening a UPS account or applying for a new one. You should contact UPS for opening an account if you don't have one.

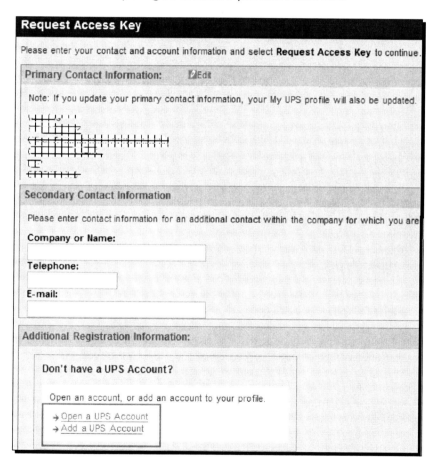

After getting the access key, we can set up UPS shipping on OpenCart.

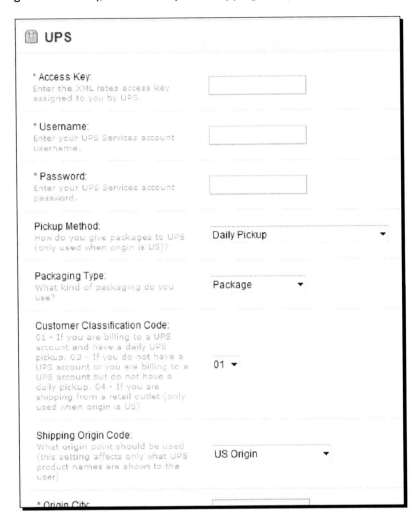

We should continue working in Test mode until we are sure that everything works as we want, because we will be charged by UPS for every order in Production mode.

USPS

USPS (United States Postal Service) is the official post office of the US government. OpenCart supports integration with USPS services. First, we should open an account using the following address:

```
https://secure.shippingapis.com/registration
```

After completion of registration, we will start working on the test server by default. Complete all tests there. After this, we will need to send an email to the email address which they sent us upon registration, stating that we need to change into production server.

After the change, we can offer USPS shipping for our customers.

Activating multiple shipping methods

OpenCart allows for activating more than one shipping option and customers can choose the most convenient one according to their needs. The following screenshot shows a sample checkout page with multiple shipping methods:

Customer Side – multiple shipping addresses

OpenCart allows customers to define more than one shipping address, but a customer can only use one shipping address per order. So, he/she has to order more than once to ship products to different addresses.

Summary

In this chapter, we have learned how to enable standard shipping options and how to begin using established package delivery companies like UPS, and USPS. As you may notice, setting up shipping methods is not difficult; the real issue deciding which method(s) to apply. Shipping is generally the most problematic area for an online business and the success is also determined by the quality of the parcel service. The aim should be to minimize the shipping problems to maximize the customer satisfaction.

In the next chapter, we will learn how to promote a store by using coupons, special bulk purchase discounts, item based discounts, etc.

7
Offering Coupons Discounts

There are many different promotion methods for an online store. The most effective methods are offering discount coupon codes on orders exceeding a defined value, setting discounts for certain products valid for a certain period of time, and even making discounts on wholesale bulk purchases. We will learn all the coupon and discount usages available in OpenCart.

In this chapter we shall learn:

- Coupon types (percentage-based, fixed amount, with free shipping)
- Applying discounts for certain products
- Applying wholesale discounts for bulk purchases

Coupons on OpenCart

Coupons are one of the most effective promotion types for an online store. These are special short texts which customers enter on the checkout page to get discounts.

For example, DISC100 could be a coupon code for a $100 discount, valid between the dates 01.08.2010 and 01.10.2010.

OpenCart supports defining several different types of coupons. Let's learn about them with examples.

Percentage-based

Sample coupon code variants are:

- Coupon code for 10 percent savings for all products
- Coupon code for 15 percent savings for all products with a minimum basket value of $200
- Coupon code for 4 percent savings on only a few selected products
- Coupon code for 8 percent savings on only a few selected products with a minimum basket value of $200

Fixed amount

Sample coupon code variants are:

- Coupon code for $25 savings for all products
- Coupon code for $35 savings for all products with a minimum basket value of $200
- Coupon code for $15 savings on only a few selected products
- Coupon code for $5 savings on only a few selected products with a minimum basket value of $200

Free shipping

Additionally, we can offer free shipping and combine it with a percentage or fixed amount based coupon:

- Coupon code for $25 savings for all products and free shipping if the order value is more than $300
- Coupon code for 15 percent savings for selected products and free shipping if the order value is more than $200

Note that every coupon code is defined with a maximum usage value in OpenCart. For example, a $20 discount coupon which can be used maximum 50 times by customers. We can even limit the coupon usage per customer. For example, a coupon code which can be used only twice per customer, so for two orders only.

Time for action – defining a 10 percent discount coupon code for orders more than $200

In this section, we will learn how to define a 10 percent discount coupon code for orders more than $200. The coupon code will be available only for a month and will be limited in numbers, which is a maximum of 10 usages. Each customer will be able to use any number of them. The coupon will be valid for all products in the store.

1. Let's open the **Sales | Coupons** menu and delete all the coupons which were set upon installation by default.

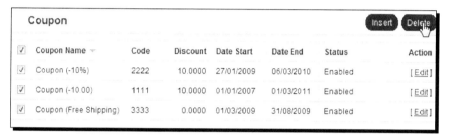

2. Then, let's click on the **Insert** button to start defining a new coupon. On the coupon edit page, we will write **10% Off** for **Coupon Name**; fill **Coupon Description**. Let's give the coupon **Code** as **OFF10200**, and choose **Type** as **Percentage**. **Discount** percentage will be **10** on **Total Amount** of **200**. We will require that **Customer Login** before applying the coupon. We will not provide free shipping with the coupon. So, we select **No** for **Free Shipping**.

3. When we scroll down the page, we see that there are other important options. We don't select any specific **Products**. So, the coupon will be valid for any product in the store. We limit the coupon validity using **Date Start** and **Date End** options. In this case, it is exactly a month.

We define that the maximum number of coupon usages is **10** by **Uses Per Coupon** field.

 A customer can even use all these maximum coupon number with 10 different orders. We have defined it with the **Uses Per Customer** field.

Finally, we have chosen the **Status** field as **Enabled**. Let's not forget to click on the **Save** button to complete adding coupon.

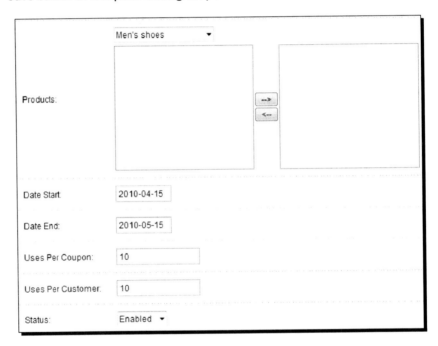

4. The following screenshot shows **before the application of coupon** on the checkout page. Notice the **Sub-Total** value of **$225**.

5. And, **after applying coupon code**. Notice that the **10% Off** coupon code only made a discount on the **Sub-Total** value. It did not affect the shipping method total.

Note that a customer **cannot** use more than one coupon for an order to get more discounts. So, he or she can choose only one from multiple available coupons per order.

What just happened?

We have learned how to apply a percentage discount on orders more than a specified value. We have noticed that coupon code did not affect final shipping cost.

Have a go hero – testing the coupon code with orders less than $200

Test what would happen if you applied the 10 percent off coupon code with a shopping cart value less than $200. What kind of message would OpenCart return to the customer?

Time for action – defining $5 discount coupon code for certain items and free shipping for orders more than $150

In this section, we will create a more complicated coupon. A customer would need to add **at least one certain type of product** and make a **shopping cart with a value more than $150** to get **$5 discount on shopping cart with free shipping**.

1. Let's open the **Sales | Coupons** menu again and insert a new coupon. Fill the text boxes and choose the options according to the following screenshot. Notice that we choose **Type** as **Fixed Amount** this time and **Free Shipping** as **Yes**.

2. Here, we apply this coupon only to **Reebok Fuego Running Shoe** product. A customer can use the coupon which is defined in **Uses Per Customer** as **1** only once.

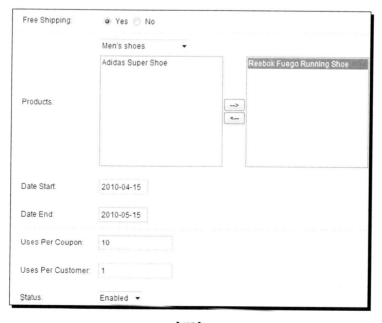

3. Let's start reviewing different customer shopping cart scenarios according to this coupon now. First of all, create another product in the store. In this case, it is **Adidas Super Shoe**. The following screenshot shows after the application coupon code for a $5 discount and free shipping. Notice that free shipping was applied even though there is **Per Item Shipping Rate** cost. This cost was totally eliminated and **$5** discount was made on product **Sub-Total** value.

4. In the following scenario, we have tried to apply a coupon code to the shopping cart where the coupon code doesn't include the certain product we defined before. Let's emphasize that we could not apply a coupon, even though the total order exceeded is $150.

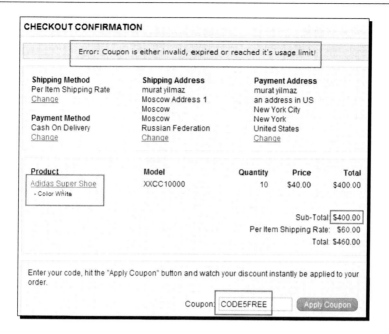

5. In the final scenario, we have added **Reebok Fuego Running Shoe** as it was included in the coupon code definition. But, again we could not apply a coupon since the total amount did not exceed $150.

What just happened?

We have learned how to define a fixed amount coupon with a minimum shopping cart limit to be activated on the customer side. Plus, applying a coupon requires putting at least one product which must be in the coupon coverage list into the basket. So, we should be very careful defining such conditional coupon codes because it can lead to customer confusion. It is wiser to create simple coupons.

Setting special discounts for selected products

Special discounts on certain products are like magnets for customers. They are encouraged to buy items with price saving opportunities. You will notice that almost all established online stores, including Amazon, apply this for a great range of products. See the following screenshot to understand how it looks on Amazon:

Time for action – applying a special low price for a product for a certain period

Now, let's learn how to apply discounts on specific products.

1. Let's open the **Catalog | Products** menu in the administration panel and edit one of the products. Then, we will need to change to the **Special** tab.

2. We will define two special discounts at once for this example, which will be run at different times. Let's notice that the first one will reduce the price to 15 for a certain period of time in April 2010. Later, it will be increased to the original price for the first 15 days of May. Then, it will be decreased again, this time to 30 after May 15.

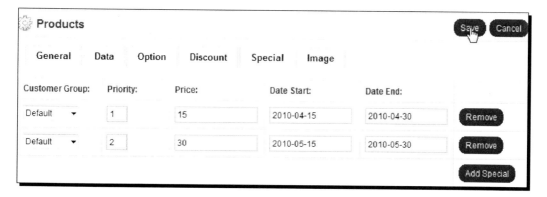

3. The following screenshot shows how it looks on the store page. Notice that the price was decreased to $15 from $45:

4. In the following case, we applied the coupon code.

 Let's understand that coupon codes and discounts are totally independent from each other. So, a customer will be able to apply coupon code even after usual product discount.

What just happened?

We have learned how easy it is to apply special discounts on products. We have also seen that we should be careful to apply discounts and coupon codes at the same time. It can lead to serious discounts on final shopping cart totals.

Discounts for wholesale

Another common practice is to apply discounts on bulk purchases.

For example, if a product is normally sold at $50, we can offer to reduce the price of one item to $20 for orders of more than 30 in quantity.

In OpenCart, we can apply such discounts even at the customer group level.

Time for action – decreasing item price to $10 for order quantities more than 40 for special wholesale customers

We will learn how to change a customer's group, and define a wholesale bulk purchase for this group. For this example, we will decrease the item price to $10 for a order more than 40 for this group.

1. Let's browse to the **Sales | Customers** menu and edit the information of a customer. We will change the **Customer Group** to **Wholesale**.

2. The next step is to open the **Discount** tab of a product. We will choose to apply the discount for **Wholesale Customer Group** for **Quantity** of **40**. The discounted **Price** will be **10**. Let's not forget to set the **Date Start** and **Date End** fields for discount validity limits.

 The priority field determines which discount to apply if there are more than two discounts falling on the same period. The discount with highest priority is valid.

3. Let's investigate different customer scenarios now.

 Let's note that we should change the customer group of a sample registration to wholesale to make the following two samples work. We can do this by using the **Sales | Customers** menu and editing a customer's group to wholesale.

In the following case, the wholesale customer cannot get a discount because the quantity is under 40:

4. In the following case, the unit price of the item was decreased to $10 since the shopping cart now has 40 of this item.

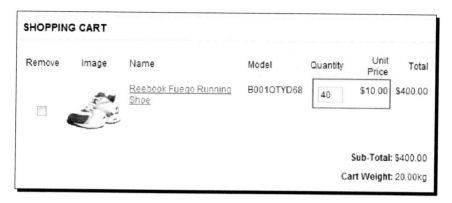

5. Let's remember that we defined another discount for **Default** grouped customers, which is $15. So, they will only see their own discounts assigned to the group, as in the following screenshot:

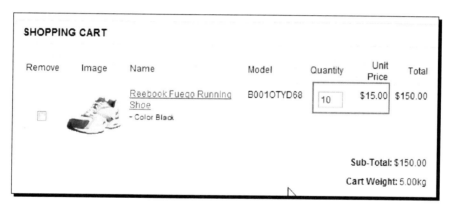

What just happened?

We have learned how to change the user group, and create a discount for a certain item which will be available only after a minimum quantity in the shopping cart. Let's also add it also that we are able to limit such bulk purchase discounts to only a certain group, as we have seen in our example.

Pop quiz – understanding coupons, and discounts

Decide whether the following statements are true or not:

1. We can create a discount coupon according to the geographical zone of the customer.

2. It is possible to define different discount rates for a certain product for different customer groups.

3. We can only offer discounts according to the total amount of the shopping cart.

Summary

In this chapter, we have learned how to define and activate coupon codes. We created coupons with fixed amounts or percentages. We could limit the usage of coupons with numbers or according to the total amount of customer shopping cart. It is also possible to offer a coupon with free shipping.

We have seen that it is also possible to create discounts on selected products for a time period. OpenCart system also allowed us to define discounts for different customer groups, such as wholesale, VIP.

In the next chapter, we will learn how to handle orders, change order statuses, and inform customers about the order statuses.

8
Understanding Order Lifecycle

OpenCart order processing is much simpler than other commercial and open source software. Eventhough the features are not advanced, they are sufficient to manage the orders successfully without headaches.

In this chapter we shall learn:

- The steps on a typical order flowchart
- Order tracking on administrative side
- Order tracking on customer side
- Generating Invoices
- Changing order statuses (Pending, Processing, Shipped, Completed)

Order flowchart

Before starting the order processing details on OpenCart, let's understand what an order flowchart is. The following flowchart shows the main possible ways from the placement of an order by customer to the completion (successful shipment) on administrative side. We have especially neglected situations about payment frauds, cancelling orders, etc. for simplicity.

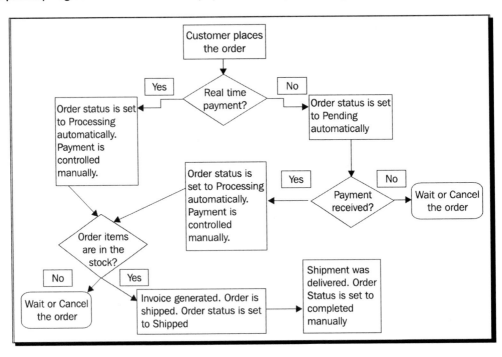

Briefly, as we can notice from the flowchart, we keep the order in **Pending** status until the payment is made (manually or automatically). If payment is made, we change the status to **Processing**. It means that we are packaging/collecting the ordered items. When we ship the order, the status changes to **Shipped**, and finally, we set it to **Completed** only after successful delivery.

This flowchart shows a typical order lifecycle. So, it is possible to change order logic, and delete/change/add new statuses according to website needs. We can edit order statuses using **System | Localisation | Order Statuses** menu.

Placing the order

The order flowchart begins with the delivery of order information by the customer on checkout pages. First of all, we collect information about **Shipping Method**, **Payment Method**, **Shipping Address**, and **Payment Address**. As we can notice from the following screenshot, shipping and payment addresses can be defined differently. So, while shipment is made to an address, invoice can be sent to another (if needed).

CHECKOUT CONFIRMATION

Shipping Method	Shipping Address	Payment Address
Per Item Shipping Rate	murat yilmaz	murat yilmaz
Change	an address in US	a germany address
	New York City	Berlin
Payment Method	New York	Berlin
Bank Transfer	United States	Germany
Change	Change	Change

We also get information about ordered products, their quantities, and the price on the order date. Note that all sub-totals are separately shown to the customer. In the following case there is a per item shipping rate, but it was cancelled by a $5 discount coupon applied with free shipping.

Product	Model	Quantity	Price	Total
Reebook Fuego Running Shoe - Color Black	B001OTYD68	2	$15.00	$30.00
Adidas Super Shoe - Color White	XXCC10000	3	$40.00	$120.00

Sub-Total:	$150.00
Per Item Shipping Rate:	$30.00
$5 Discount Coupon:	-$35.00
Total:	$145.00

The customer can also apply a coupon code for the order.

Enter your code, hit the "Apply Coupon" button and watch your discount instantly be applied to your order.

Coupon: CODE5FREE   Apply Coupon

Finally, we also get extra comments which customer can provide us. In the following case, the customer stated that he or she needs the order after a defined date.

We have also provided information about payment. In the following case, it is a bank payment:

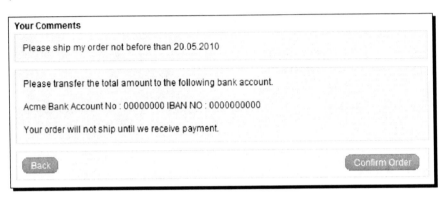

The customer is informed by the result of order confirmation on the screen:

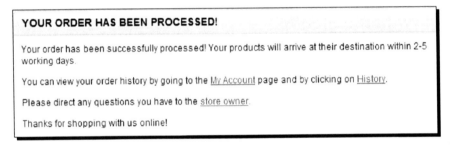

The OpenCart system generates an email according to the order and sends it automatically after the customer places the order. The following screenshot shows the sample order which the customer will get in the email box:

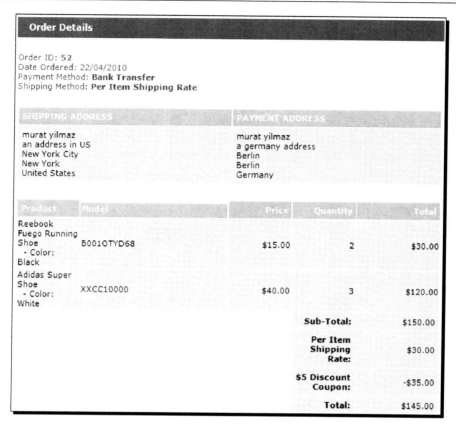

On the administration side, we see a dashboard screen after the login where we can see the latest orders, total sales, total customers, etc. There is a statistics graph which is useful to have a look at the sales, and customer trends. This graph can be generated according to the ranges such as day, week, month, and year.

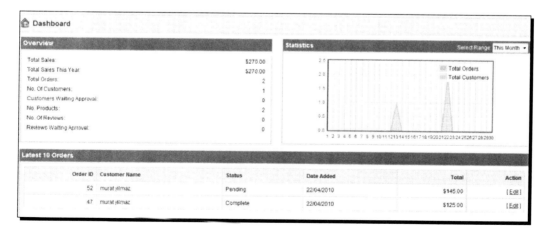

We can edit an order directly from the dashboard or by using the **Sales | Orders** menu. OpenCart shows the order details in tabs for ease of management. The following screenshot shows the first tab. The **Order Details** tab shows the **Customer** name, personal information (**email, telephone**), order date, **shipping method, payment method, order total, customer comment,** etc. Let's note that the order website is also shown. As we already know, OpenCart allows for running multiple stores on a single installation. The most important section is **Order Status**. In this case, it is set to **Pending** for new orders. Let's remember that the default value can be arranged according to each payment type. In our case, we had arranged it as **Pending** for the bank payment option since we hadn't got the payment yet.

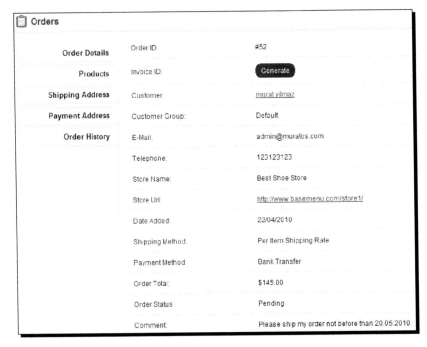

The next tab is **Products**. We see the details of ordered products and the sub-totals and total value:

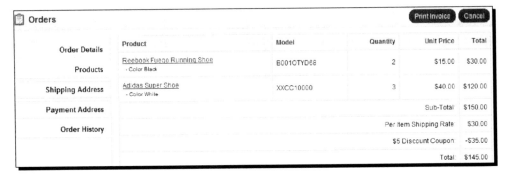

On the **Shipping Address** tab, we see the details of the shipping address:

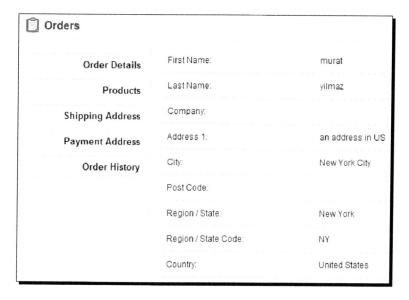

The Payment Address tab is similar to the **Shipping Address** tab. This is where we will send the invoice (if needed):

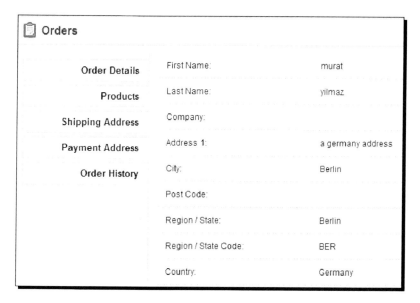

Finally, we open the most important screen for order management. The **Order History** tab shows the original order date, and status. We will track all the changes made to **Order Status** in this screen. We will also use this screen to change the **Order Status** and inform the customer by email about the changes.

Time for action – processing the order

In this section, we will learn how to complete an order step by step.

1. We have now got the payment with bank transfer. We will change the **Order Status** to **Processing** and inform the customer by checking the **Notify Customer** option. What we write in the **Comment** section will be emailed to the customer.

The following screenshot shows what the customer will get in the email inbox:

```
Order ID: 52
Date Ordered: 22/04/2010

Your order has been updated to the following status:

Processing

To view your order click on the link below:
http://www.booksbird.com/store1/index.php?route=account/invoice&order_id=52

The comments for your order are:

Thanks for the payment.

We are now processing your order.
```

This information was also recorded on the Order History page:

Date Added	Status	Customer Notified
22/04/2010	Pending	Yes

Comment

Please transfer the total amount to the following bank account.

Acme Bank Account No : 00000000 IBAN NO : 0000000000

Your order will not ship until we receive payment.

Date Added	Status	Customer Notified
22/04/2010	Processing	Yes

Comment

Thanks for the payment. We are now processing your order.

2. Suppose that we are ready to ship the order items. Now, it is time to **Generate** an **Invoice ID**. This is on the **Order History** tab as well. We can use this invoice as both a regular business invoice or/and a shipping invoice.

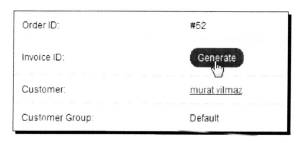

Order ID:	#52
Invoice ID:	Generate
Customer:	murat yilmaz
Customer Group:	Default

3. Now, we can **Print Invoice** on the screen. Let's remember that an invoice is a legal document and shows the payment amount and purchase of the products.

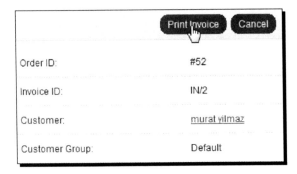

The following screenshot shows the **Invoice**. Notice the information about our store and payment and shipment addresses, an the items in the shipment, are clearly shown:

4. We should set **Order Status** to **Shipped** after real shipping is made. It is also a good practice to **Notify Customer** with a **Comment** in the email.

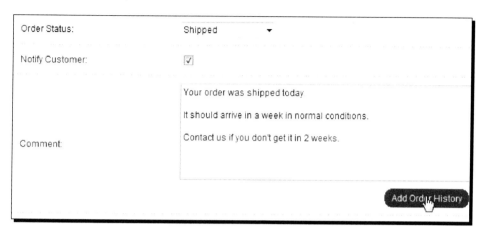

This is what a customer will see in their email about the shipping:

```
Order ID: 52
Date Ordered: 22/04/2010

Your order has been updated to the following status:

Shipped

To view your order click on the link below:
http://www.basemenu.com/store1/index.php?route=account/invoice&order_id=52

The comments for your order are:

Your order was shipped today.

It should arrive in a week in normal conditions.

Contact us if you don't get it in 2 weeks.
```

5. Suppose that we have learned that our shipping was delivered by a parcel company. It is now time to **Complete** the order. We don't need to inform the customer since they have already got the products.

6. We can trace all the steps on the processes of an order in detail on the **Order History** tab at the order details page.

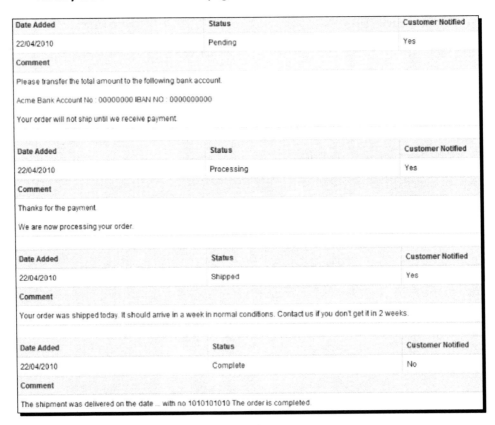

Date Added	Status	Customer Notified
22/04/2010	Pending	Yes
Comment		
Please transfer the total amount to the following bank account.		
Acme Bank Account No : 00000000 IBAN NO : 0000000000		
Your order will not ship until we receive payment.		
Date Added	**Status**	**Customer Notified**
22/04/2010	Processing	Yes
Comment		
Thanks for the payment.		
We are now processing your order.		
Date Added	**Status**	**Customer Notified**
22/04/2010	Shipped	Yes
Comment		
Your order was shipped today. It should arrive in a week in normal conditions. Contact us if you don't get it in 2 weeks.		
Date Added	**Status**	**Customer Notified**
22/04/2010	Complete	No
Comment		
The shipment was delivered on the date ... with no 1010101010 The order is completed.		

What just happened?

We have learned how to apply each order status step and inform the customer about it. The default order was **Pending** for bank payments. Step by step we have changed it to Processing, Shipped, and Completed.

Have a go hero – placing an order and canceling it

Place an order as a fictional customer and suppose that you are already paid by Paypal. Cancel the order because you don't have enough stocks for the ordered items. Look at the pre-defined order statuses and change them accordingly on each step until you refund the customer.

Pop quiz – understanding order flowchart

1. Why do we need two separate Order Status options, Shipped and Completed?

2. Can we generate an invoice and send to the customer before the payment is made?

Summary

In this chapter, we have learned how we process orders. We have learned that the only screen we will use is the **Order History** tab at order details. We can change the status of orders, add extra information about order status as comments, and notify the customer by email if needed.

In the next chapter, we will learn how to group customers, change their information, and manage them.

9
Managing Customers and Users

A store can use the most advanced online store software, apply very good competitive prices, but still be unsuccessful due to insufficient customer relationship management. Thus, solving customer problems and grouping customers in segments are key for success.

An online store owner can need more than one login to manage different tasks on the store. For example, while a user takes care of orders, another can only enter and change information for products. OpenCart basically provides the ability to create new users with different permissions.

In this chapter we shall learn about:

- Advantages of customer registration
- Important customer settings
- Grouping customers
- Sending email newsletters and messages
- Adding customer information manually
- Adding a new user group
- Assigning permissions to a group
- Assigning a user to a group
- Testing user permissions

Advantages of customer registration

Although we have a chance to accept orders without any customer registration, there are very important advantages of storing customer information in the store both for the store owner and the customer.

Advantages for a customer

Once a customer orders from the store, it will be easy to track the status of the order on the website rather than contacting the store regularly.

MY ORDER HISTORY

Order ID: #52   Status: Complete

Date Added: 22/04/2010   Customer: murat yilmaz
Products: 2   Total: $145.00   View

Order ID: #47   Status: Complete

Date Added: 22/04/2010   Customer: murat yilmaz
Products: 2   Total: $125.00   View

A registered customer can view all the details of the previous and current orders online.

Product	Model	Quantity	Unit Price	Total
Adidas Super Shoe - Color White	XXCC10000	1	$40.00	$40.00
Reebook Fuego Running Shoe - Color Black	B001OTYD68	2	$45.00	$90.00

Sub-Total: $130.00
US Shipping Zone (Weight 1.50kg): $17.00
$5 Discount Coupon: -$22.00
Total: $125.00

It will be easy to order in the future after a simple login to the system, since a customer can create multiple addresses and select the needed shipping address instead of typing it each time.

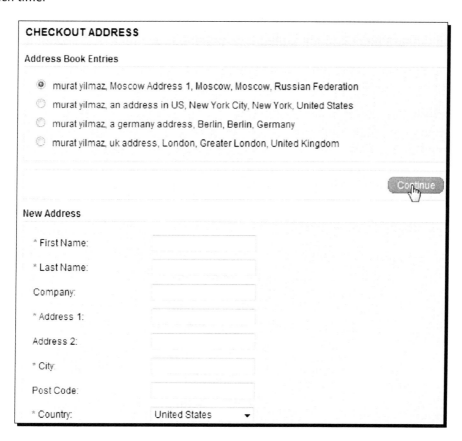

If a customer is a regular buyer from the store, store administrators can notice the customer and apply special discounts.

Advantages for the store

As a store administrator, we can analyze the customer behavior: find top paying customers, regular customers, and then apply coupons and discounts for them.

We can send regular newsletters and news about the hot deals on the store. This builds up the customer relationship.

We can group customers according to their behavior and shopping habits on the store.

Important customer settings

We have two vital settings in OpenCart which can affect the customer experience in our store, so we should consider them carefully.

The first option is whether we will require approval for new customer registrations or not.

There is no email authentication system in the OpenCart system where a registration approval email is sent to customer and he/she clicks on it to approve the account.

Instead of this, if we required approval, a store administrator would need to approve each account one by one. As soon as the account is approved, an automated email is sent to the customer informing about them of the usage. Even though reviewed approvals can reduce spam registrations greatly, it can discourage customers from further using the store, so it is not a recommended method.

The second option is whether to allow guest checkout or not. If we allow guest checkout, a customer can order from our store without registration.

Some customers still prefer guest checkout because it is faster and provides anonymity.

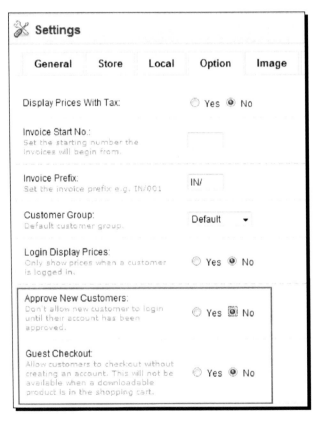

Classifying customers in groups

There are two built-in customer groups in OpenCart, Default and Wholesale. By default, all new customers are linked to the Default group. We are able to add and delete new customer groups. The following chart shows a sample customer organization:

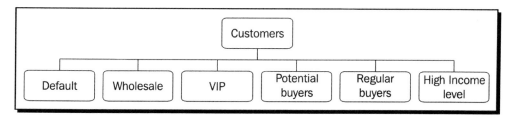

For example, if we determine that some customers are spending a lot, we can assign these customers to the **High income level** group and send them email messages about new, highly priced items in the store.

In another example, we can determine regular buyers and encourage them to spend more by sending special discount codes via email messages.

Time for action – creating a new customer group and assigning a customer to it

In this section, we will learn how to create a new customer group and assign a customer to it. By doing this, we will also cover the topic of how to edit and change a customer's information.

1. Let's open the **Sales | Customer Groups** menu and click on the **Insert** button.

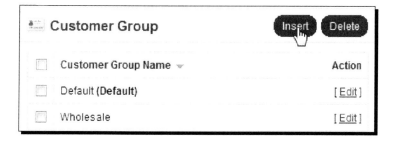

2. We will write **Customer Group Name** and click on the **Save** button to complete the operation.

3. We can browse to customer listings under the **Sales | Customers** menu and edit one of them.

4. The new customer group now is enabled in the **Customer Group** option. Optionally, we can also edit other information such as whether the customer will get a newsletter or not. We can disable a customer from loggin in to the system without deleting from the database. We click the **Save** button to complete the operation.

What just happened?

We have just learned how to create a new customer group and assign a customer to it. We have also seen that we can change important customer information such as Telephone, Email and whether a customer will get a newsletter or not.

Sending email newsletters

Email newsletter marketing is the backbone of an online store and it can greatly improve customer relationships. Offering useful product recommendations which customers can really think buying or sending product selection articles, guides is a common method. Research shows that opt-in newsletters have a high opening rate and convert better than traditional methods.

On the other hand, newsletters should be sent carefully because very frequent or irrelevant newsletters can be regarded as spam emails by customers. At the worst case, it can lead the customer to completely abandon the store for future purchases.

We can send messages to selected people by **Search** or **all newsletter subscribers** or **all customers**. Currently, OpenCart does not provide a function to send messages to selected customer groups.

 Alternatively, we can use some open source, free software to manage email newsletters for customer groups. PhpList is one of the most popular ones. There the details about it at http://www.phplist.com/.

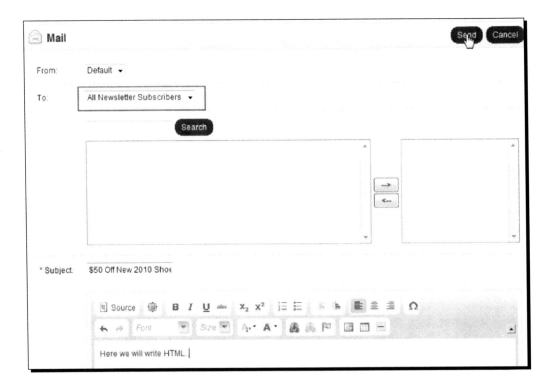

Adding customers manually

In some cases, we might need to enter customer information manually. We can achieve this by using the **Sales | Customers** menu and inserting a new customer.

 Let's remember that we are still not able to add or change customer addresses. Only a customer is able to do this by making a login to the store.

Have a go hero – creating a new customer group, assigning a customer to it, and applying a discount for this group

Start by creating a new customer group, and then assign a customer to this group. Finally, create a discount for this group and test it with sample orders.

Pop quiz – customer management

Decide whether the following statements are true or not:

1. As a store administrator, we are able to change customer addresses.
2. We are able to send email messages and newsletters according to customer group.

Users, user groups, and permissions

Users are people who do the administrative functions for our store, such as tracking sales, adding products, setting store options, and so on. They are different from customers and not related to them at all.

Users are grouped in user groups in an OpenCart system. Each group can hold more than one user and each user can have different permissions inherited by user groups.

OpenCart operates in modules. It allows us to separately assign permissions at the module level. For example, we could assign access or modify permissions for a user on **Catalog | Products** and/or **Catalog | Categories** menu.

A user with access permission can view the module information but cannot change it.

The following diagram shows a sample user (login) organization:

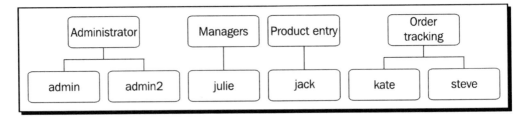

According to this diagram, we can conclude the following sample permissions:

◆ admin and **admin2** logins can do anything on the store, including changing store settings, creating products, categories, changing order status, and defining payment models.

◆ Since **Julie** is a manager, she can do everything except the things related to store and administration settings.

◆ Jack is only allowed to manage products. He can add, change, and view product information, but let's say that he cannot create a category or change order status.

◆ On the other hand, **Kate** and **Steve** can only deal with the orders while they cannot change product information and cannot add new products.

Time for action – creating a new user group, Product Entry

In this section, we will learn how to create a new user group called **Product Entry**. This group will have only permissions to view, update, and create new products.

1. Let's open the **System | Users | User Groups** menu on the administration panel.

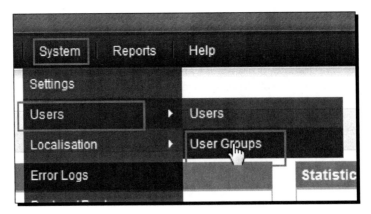

2. OpenCart has a **Demonstration** user group which is created upon installation. We don't need this. Let's delete it from the user group listings.

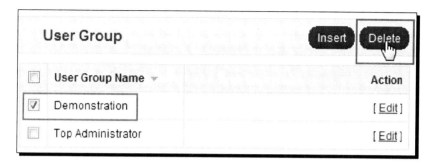

3. After the deletion, click on the **Insert** button. Then, we will need to fill in the **User Group Name** field as **Product Entry**. We select **catalog/product** from the **Access Permission** listings. Let's do the same for the **Modify Permission** listings. Let's not forget to click on the **Save** button:

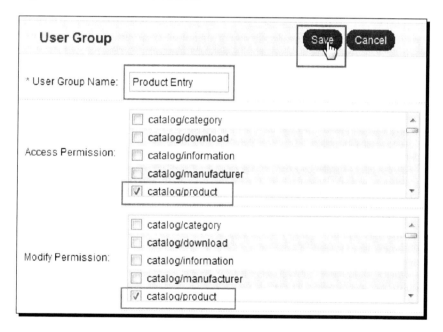

What just happened?

We have just learned how to create a new user group and assign permission to it. In this specific case, we have given permissions that are only related to product viewing, changing, and creating.

Have a go hero – creating a Manager user group

Similar to the previous section, create a user group called **Manager**. This group should have all functions (products, categories, coupons, discounts, sales, orders) except administration-related items, that is, localization.

Time for action – creating a new user and assigning to a group

In this section, we will create a new user and assign this user to the newly created Product Entry user group. Finally, we will examine the user to be sure that the user can only reach product related menus on the administration panel.

1. Let's open the **System | Users | Users** menu.

2. Let's click on the **Insert** button. Then, we will fill in the user information. Let's choose **User Group** as **Product Entry** and do not forget to change the **Status** field to **Enabled**.

3. We should now **Logout** from the system as we are using it as an **admin**.

4. Let's **login** to the administration panel with the user we have just created.

5. For example, let's try to open the **Catalog | Categories** menu.

6. As we can see in the following screenshot, we have got a **Permission Denied** error. If we try other menus except **Catalog | Products**, we will end up with the same screen.

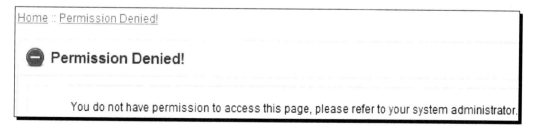

7. Now, let's browse to the **Catalog | Products** menu. As we can see from the following screenshot, we are able to use this menu. Remember that we had assigned both access and modify permissions. This lets us not only view product information but also change it or insert new products.

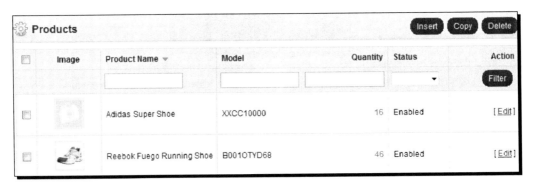

What just happened?

In this section, we have learned to create a new user assigned to a user group. In this specific case, our Product Entry group user Jack could only view and change information under the **Catalog | Products** menu. The other menus are closed to this user and he gets a **Permission Denied** message if he tries to open them.

Have a go hero – creating a new user and assigning to the Manager user group

Create a new user and then, assign this user to the Manager user group which you previously created. Test the user functionality on the administration panel, especially on changing store level permissions, such as installing a new payment module.

Pop quiz – Users, user groups

Decide whether the following statements are true or not:

1. Each user can be assigned to more than one user group on OpenCart.

2. We can create a user with view-only access to all store administration panel menus, but without the ability to change anything.

Reports

OpenCart currently provides very basic reporting functions under the Reports menu.

These are as follows:

- ◆ Sales Report, which shows the total sales between selected dates. We are able to filter out according to Date Start, Date End, Group By (days, weeks, months, years) and order statuses.

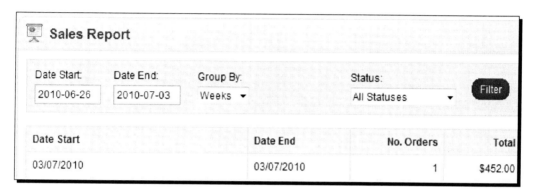

- ◆ Products Purchased Report shows the best selling products with their **quantity** and **total** amount information. However, current OpenCart report version lacks any filters like date.

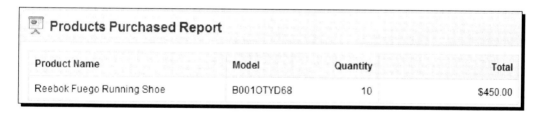

- ◆ Products Viewed Report shows the most visited products by visitors in our store and their percentages compared to all visits. Again, it is a very basic one.

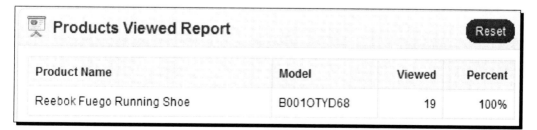

We can ask for new report modules from experienced developers on OpenCart forums or specialized OpenCart module websites.

```
http://forum.opencart.com/
http://theqdomain.com
http://www.opencartmodules.com/
http://www.opencartstore.com
```

Summary

In this chapter, we have learned why we need to group customers. We have also learned the importance of newsletters and how we send them. We have seen how to open new user logins for the administration panel working on different permission levels. This helps us to share the workload of administration with multiple people.

In the next chapter, we will learn how to add new languages and currencies for our store using localization.

10
Localization

OpenCart is open to several local customizations. It enables us to operate an online store in selected languages and with selected currencies of our choice.

In this chapter we shall learn:

- Finding and downloading a language pack
- Uploading language pack files and inserting language definitions
- Adding a new currency option
- Arranging currency exchange rates as auto-updates from the Internet

OpenCart language packs

OpenCart language packs are free contributions from the user community. After major changes on the OpenCart system, users upload new language files to `http://www.opencart.com/`. We can browse this website to find latest language packs.

Time for action – installing a new language pack

In this section, we will learn how to install a new language pack in OpenCart. For our example, we will use Swedish.

1. Let's browse into `http://www.opencart.com/` and click on the **Extensions** menu. Let's search the keyword **swedish** in the **Languages** section and then click on the **Filter** button:

2. We have found a **Swedish Capitalize to fit with screenshot language** pack. Let's browse into the **Download** tab and save the file in our computer by clicking on the **Download** button:

3. Let's extract the contents of the **swedish.zip** file to the same folder on our computer:

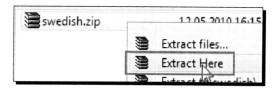

4. As we can see from the following screenshot, we have now two folders extracted; **admin** and **catalog**:

5. Let's enter into the **admin** folder. We will notice a folder named **swedish**. Let's compress it as **swedish.zip**:

6. We will do the same thing in the **catalog** folder. Let's compress the **swedish** folder as **swedish.zip** there:

7. Let's open **File Manager** in cPanel which our hosting solution has provided for us:

 Alternatively, we could use a free ftp client to upload the files. Filezilla is just one of them, freely available on `http://filezilla-project.org/`

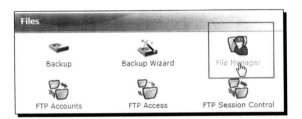

8. Let's first open the path **admin/language** in our OpenCart installation. We will see the already installed **english** folder. Let's click on the **Upload** button now:

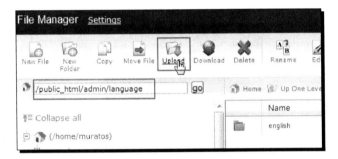

9. We should upload the **swedish.zip** file which is found in the **admin** folder to the **admin/language** folder on the server. Be careful to upload the correct `swedish.zip` file. After this, let's extract the contents of the `swedish.zip` file here by clicking on the **Extract** button:

10. We will do the same thing for the **catalog/language** folder on the server. Open this server path and click on the **Upload** button:

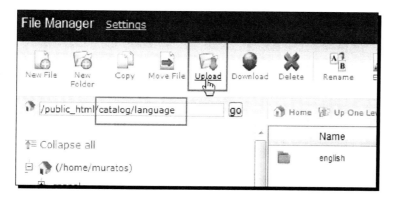

11. We will upload the `swedish.zip` file from the local **catalog** folder to the **catalog/ language** path on the server. After uploading, choose the **swedish.zip** file, and click on the **Extract** button to extract the contents here:

12. Let's log in to the administration panel. We will open the **System | Localisation | Languages** menu:

13. We already have **English** installed there by default. Let's click on the **Insert** button:

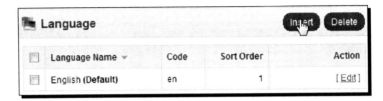

14. We will need to fill in Swedish language information as shown in the following screenshot. You can copy and paste the following field values. Finally, do not forget to select the **Status** option as **Enabled** and **Save**.

 The following information about Swedish can be found in the readme file in the archive file we had downloaded. Most language packs include such settings in a readme file as well.

Locale: **sv_SE.UTF-8,sv_SE,swedish**

Image: **se.png**

15. Let's browse into the store front and select language option as **Swedish**:

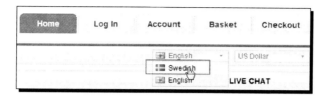

16. As we can see from the following screenshot, the store now operates in Swedish. All menu items and other definitions are changed to Swedish. Store visitors can do this at any time they want on the store front.

17. Additionally, we can arrange default local language settings in the **System | Settings | Local** menu in administration panel.

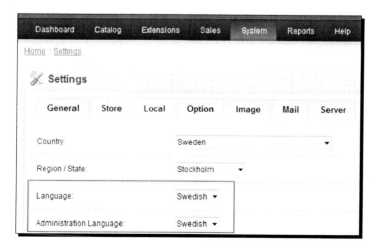

What just happened?

We have just learned where to look for different language packs for OpenCart. We have downloaded a language pack. We have separately arranged language files for admin and catalog folders. We have then uploaded them to their respective folders on the server. Finally, we have inserted the new language definition on administration panel.

Have a go hero – in running the store on your own language

Now, it is your turn to repeat these steps for your selected language. If you can't find an available language pack for your language, you can still write your own translations by editing language files on the server.

Time for action – editing the text in a language file

In this section, we will learn how to change the **Manufacturer** keyword into **Brand** on the product details page in the relevant English language file. The following screenshot shows the keyword which we will rename:

1. OpenCart has a very well designed MVC-L (Model-View-Controller-Language) based structure which helps us to easily change any files, including language files.

For coders who want to understand MVC-L software development principles more, try:

`http://en.wikipedia.org/wiki/Model-view-controller`

Other readers can continue reading the following section.

Every OpenCart URL shows the directory where related PHP files are located on web server. In our example, the product details URL is:

```
http://www.yourstore.com/store/index.php?route=product/
product&product_id=49
```

What we need to do is look at the route parameter carefully. We see that it is **product/product**. This tells us that the language file which we will edit is located under the **catalog/language/english/***product* directory on the web server and the file we should edit is `product.php`. The following screenshot shows this directory when opened by cPanel File manager. We will **Edit** this file.

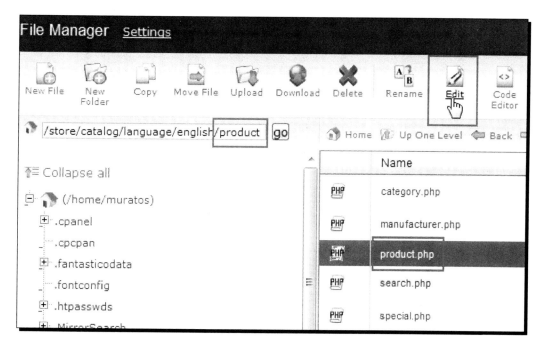

2. The system will show us a dialog box to choose the correct encoding type to edit the file. For English and most European languages, it is not very important except special characters. In any case, we select **utf-8** to not lose any characters:

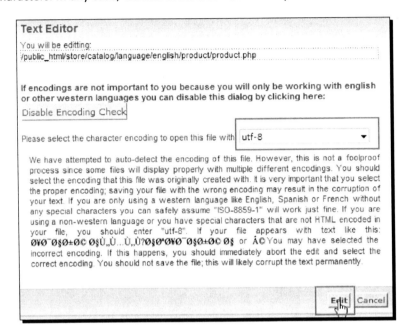

3. We find the line with **Manufacturer** text which we should replace:

```php
<?php
// Text
$_['text_enlarge']          = 'Click to enlarge';
$_['text_discount']         = 'Quantity Discount:';
$_['text_options']          = 'Available Options:';
$_['text_error']            = 'Product not found!';
$_['text_price']            = 'Price:';
$_['text_availability']     = 'Availability:';
$_['text_model']            = 'Model:';
$_['text_manufacturer']     = 'Manufacturer:';
$_['text_instock']          = 'In Stock';
$_['text_order_quantity']   = 'Order Quantity';
$_['text_price_per_item']   = 'Price Per Item';
$_['text_write']            = 'Write Review';
$_['text_no_reviews']       = 'There are no reviews for this produ
$_['text_average']          = 'Average Rating:';
$_['text_stars']            = '%s out of 5 Stars!';
$_['text_no_rating']        = 'Not Rated';
$_['text_no_images']        = 'There are no additional images for
$_['text_no_related']       = 'There are no related products for t
$_['text_qty']              = 'Qty:';
$_['text_note']             = '<span style="color: #FF0000;">Note:
$_['text_success']          = 'Thank you for your review. It has b
$_['text_wait']             = 'Please Wait!';
```

4. We change it to **Brand** and click on **Save Changes** button on the top of the screen:

```
Editing:  /home/muratos/public_html/store/catalog/language/english/    [Save Changes]
<?php
// Text
$_['text_enlarge']          = 'Click to enlarge';
$_['text_discount']         = 'Quantity Discount:';
$_['text_options']          = 'Available Options:';
$_['text_error']            = 'Product not found!';
$_['text_price']            = 'Price:';
$_['text_availability']     = 'Availability:';
$_['text_model']            = 'Model:';
$_['text_manufacturer']     = 'Brand:';
$_['text_instock']          = 'In Stock';
$_['text_order_quantity']   = 'Order Quantity';
$_['text_price_per_item']   = 'Price Per Item';
$_['text_write']            = 'Write Review';
$_['text_no_reviews']       = 'There are no reviews for this product.';
$_['text_average']          = 'Average Rating:';
$_['text_stars']            = '%s out of 5 Stars!';
```

5. When we again browse into a product detail page on the storefront, we now see our new **Brand** keyword is there:

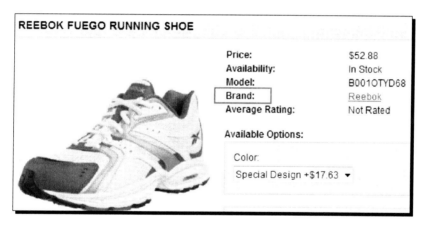

What just happened?

We have seen how to locate and edit OpenCart language files which we need to change according to the route parameter of the URL.

English storefront language files are located under **catalog/language/english**. In another language example, the path would be **catalog/language/italian** for the Italian language.

As another hint, the administration panel language files also follow the a similar pattern except that we need to browse into the **admin/language** folder instead of **catalog/language**.

Currency

OpenCart allows customers to choose from different pricing options if allowed by the store administrator. For example, you can run the store in USD, EUR, and CAD currencies.

Time for action – adding a new currency option

In this section, we will learn how to add the Canadian dollar (CAD) as a local currency option.

1. Let's browse into the **System | Localisation | Currencies** menu.

2. We will insert a new currency. Let's fill the needed fields according to the following screenshot:

3. As we can see from the following screenshot, a customer can change the currency to CAD and all prices of products will be automatically converted according to the defined exchange rate:

4. We can also set the default local currency for the store in the **System | Settings** menu, in the **Local** tab. Let's notice that there is an **Auto Update Currency** option. If we enable it, all currency exchange rates will be updated to the newest values daily:

 OpenCart gets this information from Yahoo Finance website at the backend each day, automatically.

What just happened?

We have just learned how to insert a new currency option. In this specific case, we have added a CAD option and set the exchange rate to auto-update in local store settings.

Pop quiz – localization

Decide whether the following statements are true or not:

1. We can run a store in multiple languages in OpenCart.

2. We will have to update currency rates manually every day.

Summary

In this chapter, we have learned two essential localization options. By running an online store in multiple languages, we can both impress the customers and increase the availability of website to more people. Enabling multiple currencies also can help customers to evaluate prices correctly. It is true that a store running on the local currency is more attractive to the local customers.

In the next chapter, we will learn how to check updates and correctly update to the latest OpenCart version.

11
Upgrading OpenCart

It is wise to update our OpenCart environment to the latest version regularly. It protects our system against security vulnerabilities and allows us to use new features. It is also possible that the new OpenCart version will have several bug fixes.

Moreover, new versions can have new bugs. Because of this, it is a common practice to wait while a version with major changes matures and gets rid of serious bugs with minor release fixes.

In this chapter we shall learn about:

- ◆ Making a backup of current OpenCart system
- ◆ Downloading the latest OpenCart version
- ◆ Uploading the new files to a server
- ◆ Running the upgrade script
- ◆ Checking whether everything works as expected or not
- ◆ Restoring the OpenCart system if an upgrade fails or has serious problems

This chapter is suggested reading even for an experienced user. It will show us any possible problems that might occur while upgrading, so we can avoid them.

Making backups of the current OpenCart system

One thing we should certainly do is backup our files and database before starting any upgrade process. This will allow us to restore the OpenCart system if the upgrade fails and if we cannot solve the reason behind it.

Time for action – backing up OpenCart files and database

In this section, we will now learn how to back up the necessary files and database of the current OpenCart system before starting the upgrading processes.

We will start with backing up database files. We have two choices to achieve this.

The first method is easier and uses the built-in OpenCart module in the administration panel.

1. We need to open the **System | Backup / Restore** menu.

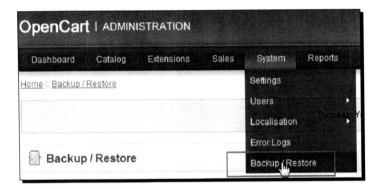

2. In this screen, we should be sure that all modules are selected. If not, click on the **Select All** link first. Then, we will need to click on the **Backup** button.

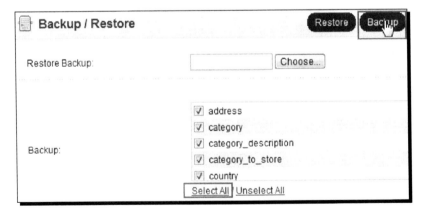

3. A **backup.sql** file will be generated for us automatically. We will **save** the file on our local computer.

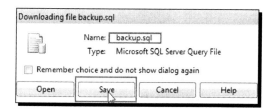

The second method to backup OpenCart database is through the Backup Wizard on cPanel administration panel which most hosting services provide this as a standard management tool for their clients. If you have applied the first method which we have just seen, skip the following section to apply. Still, it is useful to learn about alternative Backup Wizard tool on cPanel.

4. Let's open cPanel screen that our hosting services provided for us. Click on the **Backup Wizard** item under the **Files** section.

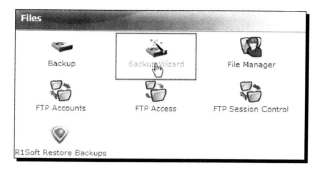

5. On the next screen, click on the **Backup** button.

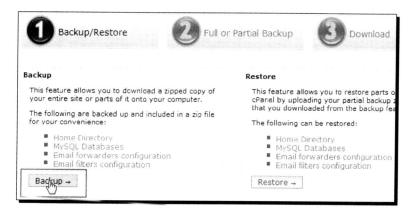

6. We will click on the **MySQL Databases** button on the **Select Partial Backup** menu.

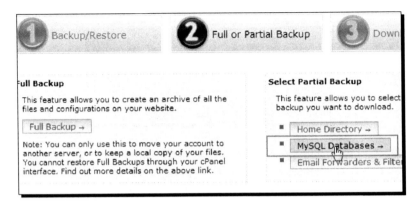

7. We will right-click on our OpenCart database file backup and save it on our local computer by clicking on **Save Link As**.

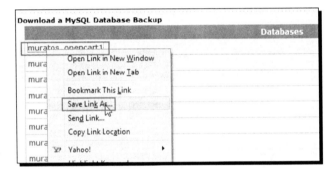

8. Let's return to the cPanel home screen and open **File Manager** under the **Files** menu.

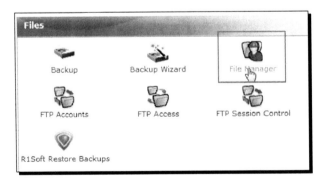

9. Let's browse into the web directory where our OpenCart store files are stored. Right-click on the directory and then **Compress** it.

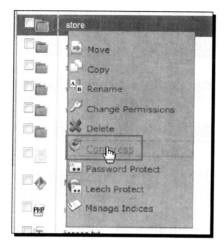

10. We will compress the whole OpenCart directory as a **Zip Archive** file.

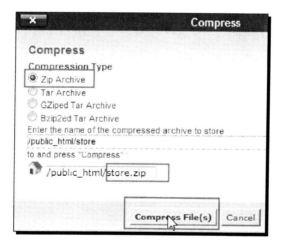

11. As we can see from the following screenshot, the compressed **store.zip** file resides on the web server. We can also optionally download the file to our local computer.

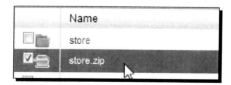

What just happened?

We have backed up our OpenCart database using cPanel. After this, we also backed up our OpenCart files as a compressed archive file using File Manager in cPanel.

New OpenCart version

Until OpenCart v1.4.7, we had to upgrade our system manually. Each new version included an `upgrade.txt` file to read first and apply upgrades manually.

For example, this is a screenshot from the v1.4.6 `upgrade.txt` file:

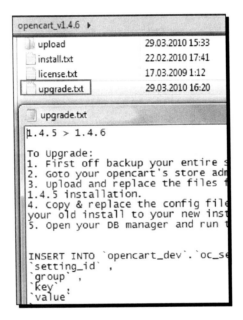

Now, starting from v1.4.7, we are able to use a universal upgrade script without opening the phpAdmin tool to execute the SQL scripts manually. The web based script supports upgrading from any version later than v1.3.0 to v.1.4.7 directly.

If we are using a version older than OpenCart v1.3.0, we will need to first upgrade all the versions in between until we reach 1.3.0. Then we can run this script.

Now, let's learn how we will use the upgrade script.

Time for action – downloading the latest Opencart files, uploading them to the server, and upgrading

We will now learn how to download the latest version of OpenCart and upload to our server. Then, we will run upgrade script.

1. Let's browse into

```
http://www.opencart.com/index.php?route=download/download
```

We will save latest OpenCart zip file on our local computer.

2. Now, let's click on the **Extract Here** menu item to extract all the contents of a folder.

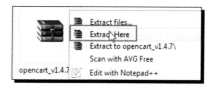

3. We need to **delete** default, and empty the **config.php** file in the **upload** folder in our **local computer**.

 Do not delete the `config.php` file on your web server by mistake.

4. We also **delete** the **config.php** file, which resides in the **upload/admin** folder in our **local computer**.

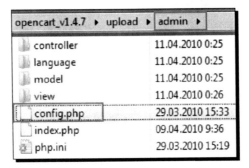

5. Now, let's add all the files in the **upload** folder into an **upload.zip** archive file on our local computer.

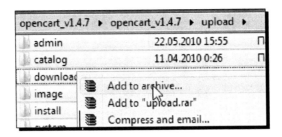

6. Let's upload the **upload.zip** file where our store files are on the web server. Then, let's **Extract** all the contents to the same folder on the web server. We should allow re-writing of all files if we get a message about doing it.

 The other solution would be deleting all files on the server except **config.php** and extracting the new files there.

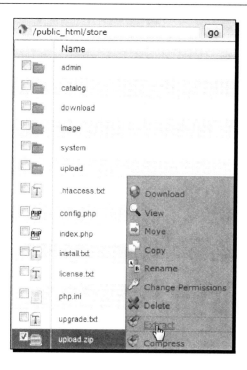

7. After the extraction is complete, let's browse into `http://www.yourwebsite.com/store/install/upgrade.php` path. Here, we have assumed our OpenCart installation is under **/store** directory. If our store files are under root folder of the website, we should browse into

   `http://www.yourwebsite.com/install/upgrade.php`.

   The script will run and inform us about the result. The following screenshot shows the success page:

8. Let's browse into the storefront now and be sure that everything is working as expected. Also, let's open the administration panel and check the system settings. If there are any changes, let's apply them to the needed settings back.

What just happened?

We have downloaded the latest OpenCart version to our local computer. We have extracted the contents of the archive file and deleted two `config.php` files which reside in the **upload** and **upload/admin** folders.

Then, we re-packaged all the upload folder content as `upload.zip`. The next step was to upload the `upload.zip` file to our webserver and extract this archive. We have re-written all files with the new versions. We have run the upgrade script and have seen the results of the upgrade process.

Finally, we have controlled all functionality of the OpenCart system, both on the storefront and on the administration panel menus.

Have a go hero – exploring config.php files

Now, go and download the `config.php` files both from the store root and admin folders. Open them with any word editor and explore the contents. They include several path definitions which OpenCart uses and your database connection information.

Restoring to the original OpenCart version

No software is completely perfect, and OpenCart is no exception. Any upgrade process can fail partially or completely. This is especially true if we have manual changes on OpenCart system files, database structure, or have used several third party mods in the system. We will now see how we will use backup files to restore our OpenCart system when needed.

Time for action – restoring OpenCart system if upgrade fails

In this section, we will now learn how to replace OpenCart files and restore the database.

1.   Let's open File Manager in cPanel and find where our OpenCart files are located. In this case, they are in the **store** folder. Let's **delete** it.

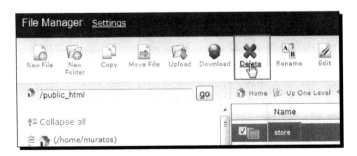

2. Let's upload our backup **store.zip** file here and **extract** the contents.

3. We now have old OpenCart files which are retrieved from the backup file, as we can see from the following screenshot:

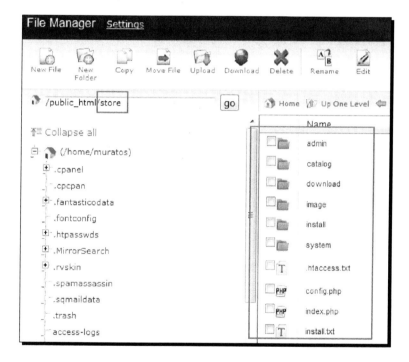

4. We can use the built-in Restore tool of OpenCart. Let's browse into the **System | Backup | Restore** menu. After that let's choose the `backup.sql` files which we have previously saved in our local computer. All we need to do finally is to click on the **Restore** button on the top of the screen.

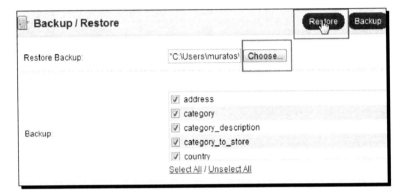

 If you have used the first method of restoring OpenCart database, you can skip the following section. Still, you can read it to increase your knowledge on cPanel Backup Wizard.

5. Let's open **Backup Wizard** on cPanel. It is under the **Files** menu.

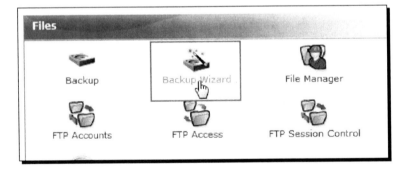

6. We will need to click on the **Restore** button to continue.

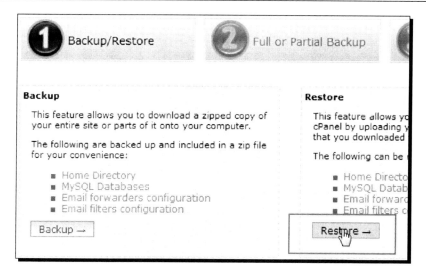

7. Let's click on the **MySQL Databases** button on the **Select Restore Type** menu.

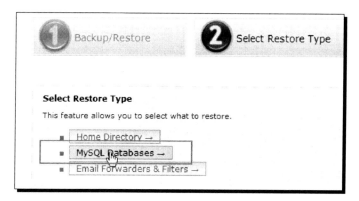

8. We will need to **browse** the OpenCart database backup file which we have already backed up before. After this, let's click on the **Upload** button.

9. The restore wizard will run the contents of the SQL file in the archive. It will drop all tables in this database, recreate them, and reinsert all of the values.

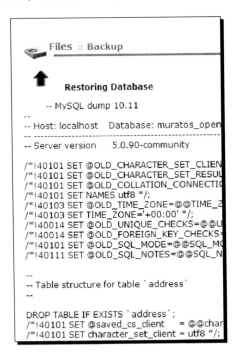

10. Now, we should check both the storefront and administration settings manually to be sure that every functionality works as expected.

What just happened?

We first deleted all OpenCart files. Then, we have uploaded the backup file and xtracted the contents. So, we have finished restoring files. We have opened the Backup Wizard in cPanel and uploaded a database backup through the wizard. It has run and overwritten our database to old values which are retrieved from the SQL backup file.

Pop quiz – understanding OpenCart upgrade process

1. Suppose that we have accidentally overwritten current `config.php` files with the empty `config.php` files which are included in new OpenCart releases. What would happen if we run the upgrade wizard?

2. Can we upgrade any OpenCart version using the latest auto-update script which we can download on the official OpenCart website?

Summary

As we can see, upgrading OpenCart is not a difficult task thanks to new upgrade script, but the upgrade process still needs a careful execution order. The most important thing is to back up files and the database beforehand. Also, we should be careful about not to overwrite working `config.php` files with the empty config files that come with new versions.

In this chapter, we learned how to upgrade OpenCart on a web server and restore the old system if an upgrade fails.

Pop Quiz Answers

Chapter 1

Uploading OpenCart Files

1	The correct answer is stated in b. Transfer utility is much faster and reliable since we need to send only one zip file and it will be extracted on server side just one click later. On the other hand, FTP client sends OpenCart files one by one and it increases the chance of interruptions on file transfer.

Chapter 2

Understanding Option Values

1	The correct answer is stated in b. It is logical to take advantage of options whenever possible. Adding a new product for every new feature would make both the management of our store and the customer experience harder.

Chapter 3

Understanding OpenCart Taxes

1	False. Each product can have only one tax class.
2	False. We can group several geo zones under one tax class.
3	False. Some products may not need any tax class. So, they can be defined as tax-free.

Chapter 4

Understanding SEO for online stores

a	True. It is wise to optimize the store for SEO and then submit to search engines for crawling. If we neglect the SEO practice for a long time and search engines already index the parametric pages; it can result in delays indexing new SEO optimized pages in good positions in search engines.
b	True. SEO URLs for categories work according to All-or-Nothing principle. This is especially true for category-subcategory relations. Forgetting to apply SEO keyword for a single category can break the store category navigation.

Chapter 5

Understanding Online Credit Card Processing

1	False. PayPal provides a merchant account for us.
2	False. We don't need to put much effort to start accepting credit cards. Payment gateways which provide a merchant account will easily enable us accepting credit cards online. PayPal and Authorize.net are two of these popular services.
3	True. PayFlow Pro does not include a merchant account.

Chapter 6

Web Based Shipping Rates Usage

1	OpenCart shows shipping cost as zero (0) in this case because it was not defined in Rates field. To overcome this problem, you can define Rates covering all possible user actions.
2	True. Weight Based Shipping method can be activated for every zone with different rates. Remember that multiple zone definitions were not possible with other methods like Flat rate, Free Shipping, Per Item etc.

Chapter 7

Understanding Coupons, Discounts

1	False. We can create coupons for all products or a selected list of products. In current version, it is not possible to create coupons according to geo zones of customers.
2	True. We can offer the same item at different prices according to customer group. OpenCart even allows us creating a new customer group. A common application would be a VIP list which buys regularly at the store. We can give more discounts for this group.
3	False. It is also possible to offer discounts according to shopping cart item quantity. It is especially used for wholesale customers who buy at bulk quantities.

Chapter 8

Understanding Order Flowchart

1	Suppose that we had shipped the orders and set Order Status as Shipped. But, what if the shipment doesn't arrive to the customer due to a problem in customs clearance? So, Shipped status only shows that the items are shipped but not the results of the shipment. So, we need Completed as a way to differentiate the result. Furthermore, we can filter orders according to Shipped status to find the problematic shipments which didn't change into Completed status after waiting for a long time.
2	It depends on what kind of scenario we will follow for our store. For example, we can generate the invoice before the payment and send the customer email address to inform about where to make the payment, for example in the case of check/money order.

Chapter 9

Customer management

1	False. Only customers can change their own addresses.
2	False. We can send email to individually selected customers, newsletter subscribers or all customers. Current OpenCart system doesn't support newsletter sending on customer group level.

Users, User Groups

1	False. Currently, each user can be a member of only one user group.
2	True. To achieve this functionality, we should create a group with all Access permission options but without any Modify permission options on User group creation screen. This method will achieve a global view-only behaviour.

Chapter 10

Localization

1	True
2	False. There is an option to auto update currency exchange rates in settings.

Chapter 11

Understanding OpenCart Upgrade Process

1	The upgrade would certainly fail, plus OpenCart would stop running. `Config.php` files include path definitions and required for OpenCart running. Upgrade wizard would try to retrieve directory information from `config.php` files but would fail since the files are empty. So, we should not forget to have backup of `config.php` files under our hands in a safe place.
2	It is false. OpenCart automatic upgrade script supports versions higher than 1.3.0. If we have an older version, we will need to first apply all upgrades individually until we reach to 1.3.0. Then, it is possible to apply the universal OpenCart upgrade script.

Index

M

manufacturers. *See* **brands**
merchant account
  about 100
  opening 100
  URL 100
Model-View-Controller-Language. *See* **MVC-L**
mod_rewrite extension 8
mod_rewrite module 79
module websites, OpenCart
  URL 182
multiple shipping methods, OpenCart
  activating 135
MVC-L
  URL 191
MySQL Database
  creating 21-24

O

online credit card processing
  about 100
  flowchart 101
online store
  about 167
  email newsletter, sending 173
OpenCart
  about, 7
  and SEO 78
  and templates 87
  archive file, downloading, 9, 10
  categories 33
  coupons 137
  customers, settings 170
  discounts, applying on customer group level
      149-151
  downloading, 9
  downloading, URL, 9
  files, uploading to web host, 10
  Geo Zones 60
  installing, 9, 10
  installing, on store directory, 10-15
  instance, adding, 31
  merchant account 100
  modules 90
  multiple shipping addresses 136

multiple shipping methods, activating 135
MySQL Database, creating, 21-23
language packs 183
localization 183
options 33
order flowchart 154
orders, accepting from countries 119
orders, shipping to selected countries 120-123
payment methods 102
permissions 175, 176
pop quiz, with answers 213-216
pricing options 194
products 33
reporting functions 181
sample online shoe store, example 34-36
tax system 59
shopping cart system 99
system, requisites, 7, 8
URL, 9
user, creating, 21-23
user group 175, 176
users 175
OpenCart, coupon types
  about 137
  example 137
  fixed-amount 138
  free shipping 138
  percentage-based 138
OpenCart archive file
  downloading, 9, 10
OpenCart files
  installation wizard, running, 29, 30
  installation wizard, using, 24-28
  permissions, setting, 19, 20
  uploading, cPanel File Manager used, 11-15
  uploading, FTP Client used, 16-18
  uploading, to web host, 10
OpenCart, installing
  about, 9
  file permissions, setting, 19, 20
  files, uploading, 10
  installation wizard, using, 24-28
OpenCart Installation Wizard
  using, 24-30
OpenCart Instance
  adding, 31

Thank you for buying
OpenCart 1.4 Beginner's Guide

About Packt Publishing

Packt, pronounced 'packed', published its first book "*Mastering phpMyAdmin for Effective MySQL Management*" in April 2004 and subsequently continued to specialize in publishing highly focused books on specific technologies and solutions.

Our books and publications share the experiences of your fellow IT professionals in adapting and customizing today's systems, applications, and frameworks. Our solution based books give you the knowledge and power to customize the software and technologies you're using to get the job done. Packt books are more specific and less general than the IT books you have seen in the past. Our unique business model allows us to bring you more focused information, giving you more of what you need to know, and less of what you don't.

Packt is a modern, yet unique publishing company, which focuses on producing quality, cutting-edge books for communities of developers, administrators, and newbies alike. For more information, please visit our website: www.packtpub.com.

About Packt Open Source

In 2010, Packt launched two new brands, Packt Open Source and Packt Enterprise, in order to continue its focus on specialization. This book is part of the Packt Open Source brand, home to books published on software built around Open Source licences, and offering information to anybody from advanced developers to budding web designers. The Open Source brand also runs Packt's Open Source Royalty Scheme, by which Packt gives a royalty to each Open Source project about whose software a book is sold.

Writing for Packt

We welcome all inquiries from people who are interested in authoring. Book proposals should be sent to author@packtpub.com. If your book idea is still at an early stage and you would like to discuss it first before writing a formal book proposal, contact us; one of our commissioning editors will get in touch with you.

We're not just looking for published authors; if you have strong technical skills but no writing experience, our experienced editors can help you develop a writing career, or simply get some additional reward for your expertise.

Django 1.2 E-commerce

ISBN: 978-1-847197-00-9   Paperback: 244 pages

Build powerful e-commerce applications using Django, a leading Python web framework

1. Build all the components for an e-commerce store, from product catalog to shopping cart to checkout processor

2. Build a high quality e-commerce site quickly and start making money

3. All the examples in the book will run smoothly for all the versions of Django 1.x

4. Follow a tutorial format to build many components from scratch while leveraging the open-source community to enhance functionality

Joomla! E-Commerce with VirtueMart

ISBN: 978-1-847196-74-3   Paperback: 476 pages

Build feature-rich online stores with Joomla! 1.0/1.5 and VirtueMart 1.1.x

1. Build your own e-commerce web site from scratch by adding features step-by-step to an example e-commerce web site

2. Configure the shop, build product catalogues, configure user registration settings for VirtueMart to take orders from around the world

3. Manage customers, orders, and a variety of currencies to provide the best customer service

4. Handle shipping in all situations and deal with sales tax rules

Please check **www.PacktPub.com** for information on our titles

open source *
community experience distilled

[PACKT]
PUBLISHING

PrestaShop 1.3 Beginner's Guide

ISBN: 978-1-849511-14-8   Paperback: 308 pages

Build and customize your online store with this speedy, lightweight e-commerce solution

1. Covers every topic required to start and run a real, trading e-commerce business with PrestaShop

2. Deploy PrestaShop quickly and easily, and make your PrestaShop search-engine friendly

3. Learn how to turn a single new PrestaShop into a thriving e-commerce empire

4. Step-by-step fully illustrated explanation and discussions aimed at helping beginners like you towards the realization of your own PrestaShop store and beyond

Magento 1.3: PHP Developer's Guide

ISBN: 978-1-847197-42-9   Paperback: 260 pages

Design, develop, and deploy feature-rich Magento online stores with PHP coding

1. Extend and customize the Magento e-commerce system using PHP code

2. Set up your own data profile to import or export data in Magento

3. Build applications that interface with the customer, product, and order data using Magento's Core API

4. Packed with examples for effective Magento Development

Please check **www.PacktPub.com** for information on our titles

Magento: Beginner's Guide

ISBN: 978-1-847195-94-4   Paperback: 300 pages

Create a dynamic, fully featured, online store with
the most powerful open source e-commerce software

1. Step-by-step guide to building your own
   online store

2. Focuses on the key features of Magento
   that you must know to get your store up
   and running

3. Customize the store's appearance to make
   it uniquely yours

4. Clearly illustrated with screenshots and a
   working example

PrestaShop 1.3 Theming – Beginner's Guide

ISBN: 978-1-849511-72-8   Paperback: 312 pages

Develop flexible, powerful, and professional themes
for your PrestaShop store through simple steps

1. Control the look and feel of your PrestaShop
   store by creating customized themes

2. Learn the tips and tricks to make theming in
   PrestaShop easier

3. Create your own PrestaShop theme in a few
   simple steps

4. Learn how to use PrestaShop back office panel
   to make simple changes to your theme as well
   as tweaking the right lines of code to customize
   the look of your store

Please check **www.PacktPub.com** for information on our titles

Lightning Source UK Ltd.
Milton Keynes UK
175097UK00002B/56/P